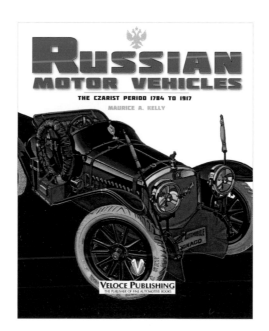

RUSSIAN MOTOR VEHICLES

THE CZARIST PERIOD 1784 TO 1917

MAURICE A. KELLY

VELOCE PUBLISHING
THE PUBLISHER OF FINE AUTOMOTIVE BOOKS

Other great books from Veloce –

Speedpro Series
4-cylinder Engine – How To Blueprint & Build A Short Block For High Performance (Hammill)
Alfa Romeo DOHC High-performance Manual (Kartalamakis)
Alfa Romeo V6 Engine High-performance Manual (Kartalamakis)
BMC 998cc A-series Engine – How To Power Tune (Hammill)
1275cc A-series High-performance Manual (Hammill)
Camshafts – How To Choose & Time Them For Maximum Power (Hammill)
Competition Car Datalogging Manual, The (Templeman)
Cylinder Heads – How To Build, Modify & Power Tune Updated & Revised Edition (Burgess & Gollan)
Distributor-type Ignition Systems – How To Build & Power Tune New 3rd Edition (Hammill)
Fast Road Car – How To Plan And Build Revised & Updated Colour New Edition (Stapleton)
Ford SOHC 'Pinto' & Sierra Cosworth DOHC Engines – How To Power Tune Updated & Enlarged Edition (Hammill)
Ford V8 – How To Power Tune Small Block Engines (Hammill)
Harley-Davidson Evolution Engines – How To Build & Power Tune (Hammill)
Holley Carburetors – How To Build & Power Tune Revised & Updated Edition (Hammill)
Honda Civic Type R, High-Performance Manual (Cowland & Clifford)
Jaguar XK Engines – How To Power Tune Revised & Updated Colour Edition (Hammill)
MG Midget & Austin-Healey Sprite – How To Power Tune New 3rd Edition (Stapleton)
MGB 4-cylinder Engine – How To Power Tune (Burgess)
MGB V8 Power – How To Give Your, Third Colour Edition (Williams)
MGB, MGC & MGB V8 – How To Improve New 2nd Edition (Williams)
Mini Engines – How To Power Tune On A Small Budget Colour Edition (Hammill)
Motorcycle-engined Racing Car – How To Build (Pashley)
Motorsport – Getting Started in (Collins)
Nissan GT-R High-performance Manual, The (Gorodji)
Nitrous Oxide High-performance Manual, The (Langfield)
Rover V8 Engines – How To Power Tune (Hammill)
Sportscar & Kitcar Suspension & Brakes – How To Build & Modify Revised 3rd Edition (Hammill)
SU Carburettor High-performance Manual (Hammill)
Successful Low-Cost Rally Car, How to Build a (Young)
Suzuki 4x4 – How To Modify For Serious Off-road Action (Richardson)
Tiger Avon Sportscar – How To Build Your Own Updated & Revised 2nd Edition (Dudley)
TR2, 3 & TR4 – How To Improve (Williams)
TR5, 250 & TR6 – How To Improve (Williams)
TR7 & TR8 – How To Improve (Williams)
V8 Engine – How To Build A Short Block For High Performance (Hammill)
Volkswagen Beetle Suspension, Brakes & Chassis – How To Modify For High Performance (Hale)
Volkswagen Bus Suspension, Brakes & Chassis – How To Modify For High Performance (Hale)
Weber DCOE, & Dellorto DHLA Carburetors – How To Build & Power Tune 3rd Edition (Hammill)

Those Were The Days ... Series
Alpine Trials & Rallies 1910-1973 (Pfundner)
American Trucks of the 1950s (Mort)
Anglo-American Cars From the 1930s to the 1970s (Mort)
Austerity Motoring (Bobbitt)
Austins, The last real (Peck)
Brighton National Speed Trials (Gardiner)
British Lorries Of The 1950s (Bobbitt)
British Lorries of the 1960s (Bobbitt)
British Touring Car Championship, The (Collins)
British Police Cars (Walker)
British Woodies (Peck)
Café Racer Phenomenon, The (Walker)
Dune Buggy Phenomenon (Hale)
Dune Buggy Phenomenon Volume 2 (Hale)
Hot Rod & Stock Car Racing in Britain In The 1980s (Neil)
Last Real Austins, The, 1946-1959 (Peck)
MG's Abingdon Factory (Moylan)
Motor Racing At Brands Hatch In The Seventies (Parker)
Motor Racing At Brands Hatch In The Eighties (Parker)
Motor Racing At Crystal Palace (Collins)
Motor Racing At Goodwood In The Sixties (Gardiner)
Motor Racing At Nassau In The 1950s & 1960s (O'Neil)
Motor Racing At Oulton Park In The 1960s (McFadyen)
Motor Racing At Oulton Park In The 1970s (McFadyen)
Superprix (Collins)
Three Wheelers (Bobbitt)

Enthusiast's Restoration Manual Series
Citroën 2CV, How To Restore (Porter)
Classic Car Bodywork, How To Restore (Thaddeus)
Classic British Car Electrical Systems (Astley)
Classic Car Electrics (Thaddeus)
Classic Cars, How To Paint (Thaddeus)
Reliant Regal, How To Restore (Payne)
Triumph TR2, 3, 3A, 4 & 4A, How To Restore (Williams)
Triumph TR5/250 & 6, How To Restore (Williams)
Triumph TR7/8, How To Restore (Williams)
Volkswagen Beetle, How To Restore (Tyler)
VW Bay Window Bus (Paxton)
Yamaha FS1-E, How To Restore (Watts)

Essential Buyer's Guide Series
Alfa GT (Booker)
Alfa Romeo Spider Giulia (Booker & Talbott)
BMW GS (Henshaw)
BSA Bantam (Henshaw)
BSA Twins (Henshaw)
Citroën 2CV (Paxton)
Citroën ID & DS (Heilig)
Fiat 500 & 600 (Bobbitt)
Ford Capri (Paxton)
Jaguar E-type 3.8 & 4.2-litre (Crespin)
Jaguar E-type V12 5.3-litre (Crespin)
Jaguar XJ 1995-2003 (Crespin)
Jaguar/Daimler XJ6, XJ12 & Sovereign (Crespin)
Jaguar/Daimler XJ40 (Crespin)
Jaguar XJ-S (Crespin)
MGB & MGB GT (Williams)
Mercedes-Benz 280SL-560DSL Roadsters (Bass)
Mercedes-Benz 'Pagoda' 230SL, 250SL & 280SL Roadsters & Coupés (Bass)
Mini (Paxton)
Morris Minor & 1000 (Newell)
Porsche 928 (Hemmings)
Rolls-Royce Silver Shadow & Bentley T-Series (Bobbitt)
Subaru Impreza (Hobbs)
Triumph Bonneville (Henshaw)
Triumph Stag (Mort & Fox)
Triumph TR6 (Williams)
VW Beetle (Cservenka & Copping)
VW Bus (Cservenka & Copping)
VW Golf GTI (Cservenka & Copping)

Auto-Graphics Series
Fiat-based Abarths (Sparrow)
Jaguar MKI & II Saloons (Sparrow)
Lambretta Li Series Scooters (Sparrow)

Rally Giants Series
Audi Quattro (Robson)
Austin Healey 100-6 & 3000 (Robson)
Fiat 131 Abarth (Robson)
Ford Escort MkI (Robson)
Ford Escort RS Cosworth & World Rally Car (Robson)
Ford Escort RS1800 (Robson)
Lancia Stratos (Robson)
Mini Cooper/Mini Cooper S (Robson)
Peugeot 205 T16 (Robson)
Subaru Impreza (Robson)
Toyota Celica GT4 (Robson)

WSC Giants
Ferrari 312P & 312PB (Collins & McDonough)

General
1½-litre GP Racing 1961-1965 (Whitelock)
AC Two-litre Saloons & Buckland Sportscars (Archibald)
Alfa Romeo Giulia Coupé GT & GTA (Tipler)
Alfa Romeo Montreal – The dream car that came true (Taylor)
Alfa Romeo Montreal – The Essential Companion (Taylor)
Alfa Tipo 33 (McDonough & Collins)
Alpine & Renault – The Development Of The Revolutionary Turbo F1 Car 1968 to 1979 (Smith)
Anatomy Of The Works Minis (Moylan)
André Lefebvre, and the cars he created at Voisin and Citroën (Beck)
Armstrong-Siddeley (Smith)
Autodrome (Collins & Ireland)
Automotive A-Z, Lane's Dictionary Of Automotive Terms (Lane)
Automotive Mascots (Kay & Springate)
Bahamas Speed Weeks, The (O'Neil)
Bentley Continental, Corniche And Azure (Bennett)
Bentley MkVI, Rolls-Royce Silver Wraith, Dawn & Cloud/Bentley R & S-Series (Nutland)
BMC Competitions Department Secrets (Turner, Chambers & Browning)
BMW 5-Series (Cranswick)
BMW Z-Cars (Taylor)
BMW Boxer Twins 1970-1995 Bible, The (Falloon)
Britains Farm Model Balers & Combines 1967-2007, Pocket Guide to (Pullen)
Britains Farm Model & Toy Tractors 1998-2008, Pocket Guide to (Pullen)
British 250cc Racing Motorcycles (Pereira)
British Cars, The Complete Catalogue Of, 1895-1975 (Culshaw & Horrobin)
BRM – A Mechanic's Tale (Salmon)
BRM V16 (Ludvigsen)
BSA Bantam Bible, The (Henshaw)
Bugatti Type 40 (Price)
Bugatti 46/50 Updated Edition (Price & Arbey)
Bugatti T44 & T49 (Price & Arbey)
Bugatti 57 2nd Edition (Price)
Caravans, The Illustrated History 1919-1959 (Jenkinson)
Caravans, The Illustrated History From 1960 (Jenkinson)
Carrera Panamericana, La (Tipler)
Chrysler 300 – America's Most Powerful Car 2nd Edition (Ackerson)
Chrysler PT Cruiser (Ackerson)
Citroën DS (Bobbitt)
Classic British Car Electrical Systems (Astley)
Cliff Allison – From The Fells To Ferrari (Gauld)
Cobra – The Real Thing! (Legate)
Concept Cars, How to illustrate and design (Dewey)
Cortina – Ford's Bestseller (Robson)
Coventry Climax Racing Engines (Hammill)
Daimler SP250 New Edition (Long)
Datsun Fairlady Roadster To 280ZX – The Z-Car Story (Long)
Diecast Toy Cars of the 1950s & 1960s (Ralston)
Dino – The V6 Ferrari (Long)
Dodge Challenger & Plymouth Barracuda (Grist)
Dodge Charger – Enduring Thunder (Ackerson)
Dodge Dynamite! (Grist)
Donington (Boddy)
Draw & Paint Cars – How To (Gardiner)
Drive On The Wild Side, A – 20 Extreme Driving Adventures From Around The World (Weaver)
Ducati 750 Bible, The (Falloon)
Ducati 860, 900 And Mille Bible, The (Falloon)
Dune Buggy, Building A – The Essential Manual (Shakespeare)
Dune Buggy Files (Hale)
Dune Buggy Handbook (Hale)
Edward Turner: The Man Behind The Motorcycles (Clew)
Fast Ladies – Female Racing Drivers 1888 to 1970 (Bouzanquet)
Fiat & Abarth 124 Spider & Coupé (Tipler)
Fiat & Abarth 500 & 600 2nd Edition (Bobbitt)
Fiats, Great Small (Ward)
Fine Art Of The Motorcycle Engine, The (Peirce)
Ford F100/F150 Pick-up 1948-1996 (Ackerson)
Ford F150 Pick-up 1997-2005 (Ackerson)
Ford GT – Then, And Now (Streather)
Ford GT40 (Legate)
Ford In Miniature (Olson)
Ford Model Y (Roberts)
Ford Thunderbird From 1954, The Book Of The (Long)
Formula 5000 Motor Racing, Back then ... and back now (Lawson)
Forza Minardi! (Vigar)
Funky Mopeds (Skelton)
Gentleman Jack (Gauld)
GM In Miniature (Olson)
GT – The World's Best GT Cars 1953-73 (Dawson)
Hillclimbing & Sprinting – The Essential Manual (Short & Wilkinson)
Honda NSX (Long)
Intermeccanica – The Story of the Prancing Bull (McCredie & Reisner)
Jaguar, The Rise Of (Price)
Jaguar XJ-S (Long)
Jeep CJ (Ackerson)
Jeep Wrangler (Ackerson)
John Chatham - 'Mr Big Healey' – The Official Biography (Burr)
Karmann-Ghia Coupé & Convertible (Bobbitt)
Lamborghini Miura Bible, The (Sackey)
Lambretta Bible, The (Davies)
Lancia 037 (Collins)
Lancia Delta HF Integrale (Blaettel & Wagner)
Land Rover, The Half-ton Military (Cook)
Laverda Twins & Triples Bible 1968-1986 (Falloon)
Lea-Francis Story, The (Price)
Lexus Story, The (Long)
little book of smart, the New Edition (Jackson)
Lola – The Illustrated History (1957-1977) (Starkey)
Lola – All The Sports Racing & Single-seater Racing Cars 1978-1997 (Starkey)
Lola T70 – The Racing History & Individual Chassis Record 4th Edition (Starkey)
Lotus 49 (Oliver)
Marketingmobiles, The Wonderful Wacky World Of (Hale)
Mazda MX-5/Miata 1.6 Enthusiast's Workshop Manual (Grainger & Shoemark)
Mazda MX-5/Miata 1.8 Enthusiast's Workshop Manual (Grainger & Shoemark)
Mazda MX-5 Miata: The Book Of The World's Favourite Sportscar (Long)
Mazda MX-5 Miata Roadster (Long)
Maximum Mini (Booij)
MGA (Price Williams)
MGB & MGB GT– Expert Guide (Auto-doc Series) (Williams)
MGB Electrical Systems Updated & Revised Edition (Astley)
Micro Caravans (Jenkinson)
Micro Trucks (Mort)
Microcars At Large! (Quellin)
Mini Cooper – The Real Thing! (Tipler)
Mitsubishi Lancer Evo, The Road Car & WRC Story (Long)
Montlhéry, The Story Of The Paris Autodrome (Boddy)
Morgan Maverick (Lawrence)
Morris Minor, 60 Years On The Road (Newell)
Moto Guzzi Sport & Le Mans Bible, The (Falloon)
Motor Movies – The Posters! (Veysey)
Motor Racing – Reflections Of A Lost Era (Carter)
Motorcycle Apprentice (Cakebread)
Motorcycle Road & Racing Chassis Designs (Noakes)
Motorhomes, The Illustrated History (Jenkinson)
Motorsport In colour, 1950s (Wainwright)
Nissan 300ZX & 350Z – The Z-Car Story (Long)
Nissan GT-R Supercar: Born to race (Gorodji)
Off-Road Giants! – Heroes of 1960s Motorcycle Sport (Westlake)
Pass The Theory And Practical Driving Tests (Gibson & Hoole)
Peking To Paris 2007 (Young)
Plastic Toy Cars Of The 1950s & 1960s (Ralston)
Pontiac Firebird (Cranswick)
Porsche Boxster (Long)
Porsche 356 (2nd Edition) (Long)
Porsche 908 (Födisch, Neßhöver, Roßbach, Schwarz & Roßbach)
Porsche 911 Carrera – The Last Of The Evolution (Corlett)
Porsche 911R, RS & RSR, 4th Edition (Starkey)
Porsche 911 – The Definitive History 1963-1971 (Long)
Porsche 911 – The Definitive History 1971-1977 (Long)
Porsche 911 – The Definitive History 1977-1987 (Long)
Porsche 911 – The Definitive History 1987-1997 (Long)
Porsche 911 – The Definitive History 1997-2004 (Long)
Porsche 911SC 'Super Carrera' – The Essential Companion (Streather)
Porsche 914 & 914-6: The Definitive History Of The Road & Competition Cars (Long)
Porsche 924 (Long)
Porsche 928 (Long)
Porsche 944 (Long)
Porsche 964, 993 & 996 Data Plate Code Breaker (Streather)
Porsche 993 'King Of Porsche' – The Essential Companion (Streather)
Porsche 996 'Supreme Porsche' – The Essential Companion (Streather)
Porsche Racing Cars – 1953 To 1975 (Long)
Porsche Racing Cars – 1976 To 2005 (Long)
Porsche – The Rally Story (Meredith)
Porsche: Three Generations Of Genius (Meredith)
RAC Rally Action! (Gardiner)
Rallye Sport Fords: The Inside Story (Moreton)
Redman, Jim – 6 Times World Motorcycle Champion: The Autobiography (Redman)
Rolls-Royce Silver Shadow/Bentley T Series Corniche & Camargue Revised & Enlarged Edition (Bobbitt)
Rolls-Royce Silver Spirit, Silver Spur & Bentley Mulsanne 2nd Edition (Bobbitt)
Russian Motor Vehicles (Kelly)
RX-7 – Mazda's Rotary Engine Sportscar (Updated & Revised New Edition) (Long)
Scooters & Microcars, The A-Z Of Popular (Dan)
Scooter Lifestyle (Grainger)
Singer Story: Cars, Commercial Vehicles, Bicycles & Motorcycle (Atkinson)
SM – Citroën's Maserati-engined Supercar (Long & Claverol)
Speedway – Motor Racing's Ghost Tracks (Collins & Ireland)
Subaru Impreza: The Road Car And WRC Story (Long)
Supercar, How To Build your own (Thompson)
Tales from the Toolbox (Oliver)
Taxi! The Story Of The 'London' Taxicab (Bobbitt)
Tinplate Toy Cars Of The 1950s & 1960s (Ralston)
Toleman Story, The (Hilton)
Toyota Celica & Supra, The Book Of Toyota's Sports Coupés (Long)
Toyota MR2 Coupés & Spyders (Long)
Triumph Bonneville!, Save the – The inside story of the Meriden workers' co-op (Rosamund)
Triumph Motorcycles & The Meriden Factory (Hancox)
Triumph Speed Twin & Thunderbird Bible (Woolridge)
Triumph Tiger Cub Bible (Estall)
Triumph Trophy Bible (Woolridge)
Triumph TR6 (Kimberley)
Unraced (Collins)
Velocette Motorcycles – MSS To Thruxton Updated & Revised (Burris)
Virgil Exner – Visioneer: The Official Biography Of Virgil M Exner Designer Extraordinaire (Grist)
Volkswagen Bus Book, The (Bobbitt)
Volkswagen Bus Or Van To Camper, How To Convert (Porter)
Volkswagens Of The World (Glen)
VW Beetle Cabriolet (Bobbitt)
VW Beetle – The Car Of The 20th Century (Copping)
VW Bus – 40 Years Of Splitties, Bays & Wedges (Copping)
VW Bus Book, The (Bobbitt)
VW Golf: Five Generations Of Fun (Copping & Cservenka)
VW – The Air-cooled Era (Copping)
VW T5 Camper Conversion Manual (Porter)
VW Campers (Copping)
Works Minis, The Last (Purves & Brenchley)
Works Rally Mechanic (Moylan)

From Veloce Publishing's new imprints:

Battle Cry!
Soviet General & field rank officers uniforms: 1955 to 1991 (Streather)

Hubble & Hattie
Winston, The dog who loved me (Klute)

www.veloce.co.uk

First published in June 2009 by Veloce Publishing Limited, 33 Trinity Street, Dorchester DT1 1TT, England. Fax 01305 268864/e-mail info@veloce.co.uk/web www.veloce.co.uk or www.velocebooks.com.
ISBN: 978-1-84584-213-0 UPC: 6-36847-04213-4

Readers with ideas for automotive books, or books on other transport or related hobby subjects, are invited to write to the editorial director of Veloce Publishing at the above address.
British Library Cataloguing in Publication Data – A catalogue record for this book is available from the British Library. Typesetting, design and page make-up all by Veloce Publishing Ltd on Apple Mac.
Printed in India by Replika Press.

RUSSIAN MOTOR VEHICLES

THE CZARIST PERIOD 1784 TO 1917

MAURICE A. KELLY, C.ENG R.R.S., M.N. (RET'D)

in association with
The Michael Sedgwick Trust

VELOCE PUBLISHING
THE PUBLISHER OF FINE AUTOMOTIVE BOOKS

RUSSO-BALT K 12/15

CONTENTS

Frontispiece. The Russo-Baltic model K 12/15. An
artist's impression of the surviving car on show in the
Polytechnical Museum in Moscow.

ACKNOWLEDGEMENTS

The illustrations in this work, where specified, have been drawn by A. Zakarov, Soviet technical artist, and are reproduced with written permission from the former Trade Organization of the Soviet Union, V/O Avtoexport, 14 Ul. Volkhonka, 11992 Moscow.

Other photographs etc. have been supplied by, and are reproduced with permission from, Nikolai Nemirovich, Reference Director of the Polytechnical Museum of the former USSR, Moscow.

The author is indebted to the following individuals and organisations for their kind assistance and for the supply of documentation and illustrations etc.

NB. As the research for this work has now been conducted over many years, some of the organisations no longer exist. Such organizations will be identified by an asterisk.

Individuals:
George Avramidis Esq, Athens, Greece.
Messrs. Bishop and Mounteney of the United Machinery Organisation, Letchworth, Herts.*
Heloïse Darbyshire for typing up the manuscript and putting it on disk.
Erik van IngenSchenau Esq., Amsterdam, The Netherlands.
Nicholas Kelly BA (Lond.) for assistance with the photography etc.
Nikolai Nemirovich Esq., Reference Director, The Polytechnical Museum of the former USSR, Moscow.
Messrs. Tsunkanov & Komarovsky of the former Russian Trade Delegation, Highgate, London.*

Museums:
The staff of the Museum of Cosmonautics and Aviation, Moscow.
The staff of the Museum of the Armed Forces of the USSR, Moscow.
The staff of the Hall of Technical and Economic Achievements, St Petersburg (formerly Leningrad).
The staff of the Lenin Museum, St Petersburg (formerly Leningrad).
The trustees of the British Museum, Bloomsbury, London.
The librarian of the Montagu Motor Museum, Beaulieu, Hants.

Libraries:
The staff of the Lenin Library, Moscow.
The staff of the Intellectual Property Section of the British Library, St. Pancras, London.
The staff of the Bibliothéque National, Paris.
The staff of the Office National de la Propriété Industrielle, Paris.

Organisations:
V/O Avtoexport, Volkhonka, Moscow.*
V/O Traktoroexport, Smolenskaya, Moscow.*
Novosti Press Agency, Kensington, London.

Others:
The editor of *Motor* magazine, Temple Press Ltd London.* (Now incorporated into *Autocar*, Haymarket Publications, London.)
Also to Intourist, Moscow for arranging for an Ilyushin-62 airliner to come to London to take the writer to Moscow in February 1972.

THE MICHAEL SEDGWICK TRUST
This work is published with the financial assistance of the Michael Sedgwick Memorial Trust. This Trust was founded in memory of the famous motoring researcher and author, Michael Sedgwick, 1926-1983.
The Trust is a registered charity (Charity no. 290841) set up to encourage the publication of new motoring research and the recording of motoring history. Full details and contact address can be found on the Trust's web site,
www.michaelsedgwicktrust.co.uk
The Trust welcomes suggestions for new projects, and financial donations to help with future work.

PREFACE

It was said during the late 19th and early 20th century that "the Russians did not make good engineers," and this line of thought pervaded Western outlooks for a long time. However, this thinking was totally stupid, for scientists such as Lomonosov, Mendeleev and Tsiolkovsky contributed a vast amount of theoretical knowledge of great international benefit. The latter evaluated the parameters of space travel and rocketry, whilst Sergei Korolev and Valentin Glushko translated his ideas into reality.

In Czarist days, the Russo-Baltic Waggon Works in Riga built the world's first four-engined aircraft and put it into series production, came first in the Monte Carlo Rally of 1912, and constructed passenger cars of exceptional quality as well as rugged truck models. During the Soviet era the aftermath of World War I and the subsequent internal hostilities caused a hiatus in all sections of industry and progress was made in the motor industry only with the help of Henry Ford and other moguls from the USA and also Germany. This policy did not foster indigenous products but favoured licenced building of foreign vehicles. However, during the 1930s following the first five-year plan, the Soviets gradually evolved domestic technology in the motor vehicle manufacturing arena, and from 1928 onwards did make some very interesting products. Some talented designers, such as Andrei Lipgart and the body stylist Boris Lebedev, came to the fore in the immediate post-World War II period to produce innovative designs.

The fact that Andrei Lipgart's GAZ-M20 Pobeda saloon was the first passenger car of new design to be produced in the world during the late 1940s owing little or nothing to pre-World War II influence, is a tribute to the progress made within Soviet industry in a span of 20 years. Also, in 1924 the AMO Plant in Moscow managed to make a small batch of F-15 1½-ton trucks to be the foundation of the commercial vehicle side of manufacturing; 13 years later in 1937, the Soviet Union was one of the the largest builders of such vehicles in the world, second only to the United States of America.

All of this historical background took the interest of the writer, and he resolved to fill the gap in the documentation of the motor vehicle regarding the lack of reference to Russian products, Czarist and Soviet. The narrative commences with the early efforts of the few pioneers from 1784 onwards through the 19th century to the creation of the motor industry of the USSR in the early 1930s.

MAURICE A. KELLY
Member of the NEWCOMEN SOCIETY
Formerly 2ⁿᵈ Engineering Officer,
the ROYAL RESEARCH SERVICE
& the BRITISH MERCHANT NAVY
Chief Engineer Officer,
MARINA MERCANTE de REPUBLICA de PANAMA

PUBLISHER'S NOTE
Illustrations of early Russian vehicles are extremely rare. Some relatively poor images – for which there are no better substitutes – have been included in this work. Such pictures are still helpful to this book's aim of providing as much information as possible on an area of automotive history about which little was previously known outside the Soviet bloc.

I. INTRODUCTION

This introduction traces the experimentation that took place from the end of the 18th century and through the 19th century, until a true motor industry was founded in Imperial Russia during the early 1900s. Whilst there were few pioneers prior to 1896, those that managed to produce viable machines showed a great degree of ingenuity.

The first of these pioneers appeared at the latter end of the 18th century, and while he did not make a mechanically propelled vehicle using an outside source, such as steam or internal combustion, he did lay down principles for an adequate transmission system.

From contemporary reports and later writings and research it would appear that the first machine designed for transportation on 'common roads' in Russia that did not utilise animal power for locomotion was the 'manumotive' vehicle, thought out and constructed by Ivan Petrovich Kulibin (1735-1818) in the late 1700s. This ingenious carriage was given the name 'Camokatka' (self-drive), and work commenced upon it between 1784 and 1786. It was completed by 1791, and some trials at the time were reported to have been successful, with a speed of 28 versts/400 sadzhen per hour being recorded. (This was an old Czarist Imperial measurement that translates as 30kmh, or about 18mph.)

The carriage, which is illustrated in Fig. 1, required two people to manage it: a footman to actually propel the machine and the passenger to steer it. The footman stood on two pedals, mounted behind the seat, and he held on to a bar attached to its back panel; by pressing down alternately on each pedal, the drive was transmitted by bell-cranks and levers, via gearing, to the hind wheel on the right hand side. From the drawing it may be deduced that the main drive wheel situated behind the passenger seat was put into motion by means of a ratchet and pawl system from the bell-crank rods, and that the shaft from this main wheel carried bevel gearing which meshed with another bevel wheel fitted to a drum which may have contained some sort of brake. The form of steerage is not clear in the drawing, but presumably, a simple tiller method (as used on bath chairs) turned the single front wheel. The road wheels, which were of the traditional wooden artillery style, were quoted as being 4.25 'arshin' in diameter at the rear, and 2.25 'arshin' in front; the Czarist 'arshin' measurement was roughly one foot in length. The major material using parts for the bodywork and wheels was, of course, wood, but there were several metal parts incorporated in the design, such as the gearing, the spindles and bearings and so on.

Today, the word 'Kulibin' is used to describe anyone who is an enthusiastic amateur inventor in Russia, and this appellation justifies keeping the pioneer's memory alive.

Following the efforts of Kulibin, not much more work was apparent in the road transport field in the country and this was due to two factors. Firstly, in the Czarist Romanov era there was not much incentive given to entrepreneurs to engage in industrial pursuits, and in many cases the pastime of invention and research was left in the hands of dedicated amateurs. Consequently, varied and sometimes curious pieces of machinery resulted from the labours of the Russian pioneers. Secondly, due to the vastness of the land mass of Russia there was more need for a rail network in the 19th century than there was for a system of roads.

Unfortunately, a great deal of unimaginative criticism has appeared in the West concerning the Russian pioneers and their labours, and this has come about due to the efforts of the Soviet propagandists, who made spurious claims for all manner of inventions that were, undoubtedly, developed elsewhere. However, the facts are that many Russian scientists and inventors came to similar conclusions and results as their counterparts abroad. For example, the TV system that was perfected by Baird in Hastings in 1928 was based upon the original work of a Russian. Also, Captain Kostovics, an aviation pioneer, built an internal combustion engine of novel design using rocking beams, which was capable of driving airships in the 1880s; this unit still exists in the Museum of Aviation in Moscow, and the flight of the airship is also documented and accepted internationally. Therefore it will come as no surprise to the reader to find people who were interested in making self-propelled engines and related agricultural machinery in the 19th century, and details of one or two of these pioneers have come to light.

Two schemes that were proposed during the 1830s, but which did not come to fruition, were made firstly by K. Jankevich in 1830 and latterly by V. Guryev in 1835. These two schemes were apparently similar, but that of Guryev has the better documentation. Guryev's ideas took the form of a large carriage driven by steam, very much like those of the English inventor Hancock, but having wheels with a very broad tread. This steam carriage could draw a trailer, and an artist's impression of the carriage was made at the time. Guryev also published a map of Russia showing a network of roads linking all of the major towns. Nevertheless, this remained just a

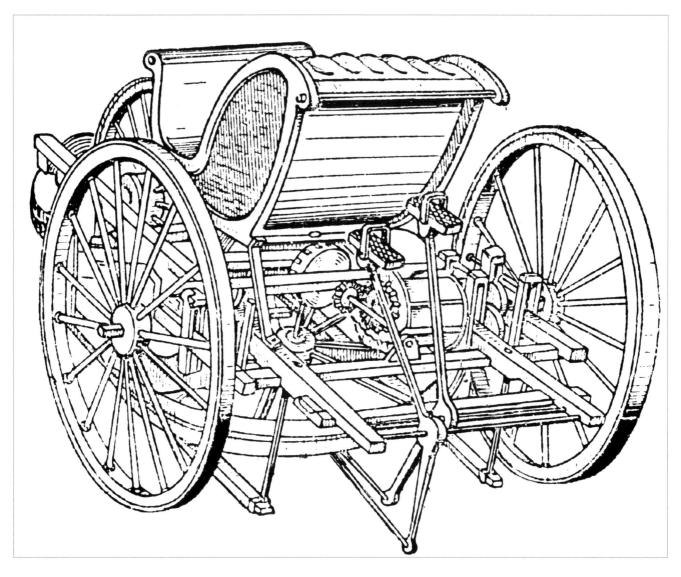

Fig. 1. Line drawing depicting Kulibin's 'Manumotive' vehicle.

scheme and it was left to promoters of the railway to establish a proper country-wide network.

The railway engineer Cherepanov made the first domestically produced steam railway locomotive in Imperial Russia after observing a similar machine built by George Stephenson at work; this engine was a four-wheeler, similar to others of the period, and it was constructed in 1835. The Cherepanov machine was built at Nizhni-Tagil in the Urals, and it had un-coupled wheels of equal diameter, cylinders set inside the frame and a very long chimney to provide adequate draught for the fire. It was of the 2-2-0 configuration.

This original steam railway locomotive heralded the start of a large rail network building enterprise in Russia which, eventually, became the largest system in the world, as well as

encompassing the greatest numerical class of steam locomotives ever made, the Class 'E' 0-10-0 of which, approximately, 11,000 units were manufactured between 1912 and 1957.

Later on, other workers, including A. Vradii and his son P. Vradii of St. Petersburg, constructed self-moving steam engines for use on the ordinary roads. In Fig. 2, a four-wheel drive steam road engine built by A Vradii is depicted; this machine was said to have been made in the 1860s and it shows considerable sophistication in its design for a machine of the mid-19th century. The power unit was enclosed within a box beneath the driver's position and it drove a jackshaft arrangement via a disengaging pinion under the control of the operator. A link-chain and sprockets drove the front wheels very much in the manner of the Lansing Steam Tractor from the USA, which was advertised

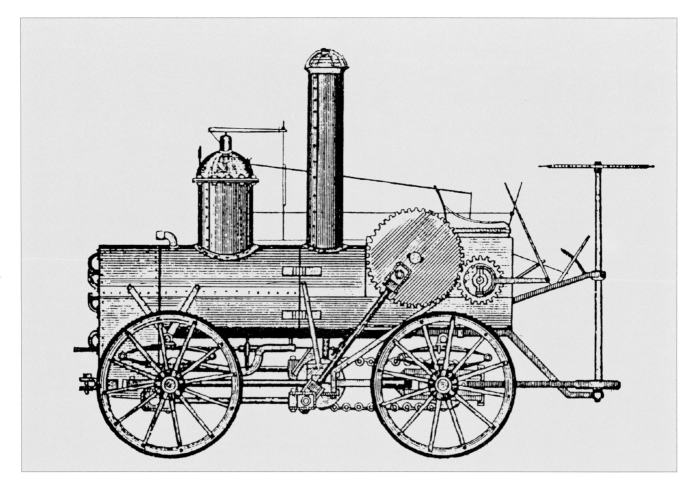

Fig. 2. Early form of steam tractor with a four-wheel drive system, manufactured by A Vradii of St. Petersburg in the 1860s.

by the Lansing Engine & Ironworks of Ingham County, Lansing, Michigan during the 1870s and 1880s. Coupling rods provided power for the hind axle; the front wheels pivoted about a central pin but were free to be driven and steered simultaneously. The whole ensemble was suspended on full elliptical springing, and at the front end the driving cum steering layout was mounted upon a separate sub-frame. Unfortunately, no details seem to be available concerning the power of this tractor, its working pressure and its dimensions etc., but it was a novel machine for its day.

Another, similar engine for traversing ice, and based on A. Vradii's engine, was made by his son, P. Vradii, and this is shown in Fig. 3. The writer is, however, slightly suspicious about the dates of construction for these engines as similar arrangements were patented in the USA in the following decade of the 19th century. One such specification was deposited at the United States Patent Office and was sealed by Riley P. Doan in 1875 (US Patent No. 158923 of 19th January 1875, "Improvements in Traction Engines").

In the summer of 1876 some experiments in road traction were made at Tsarskoe Selo, near the Czar's palace, just outside the city of St. Petersburg, and these tests were designed to show the viability of traction engines for military purposes. The Russian authorities had purchased two British engines, an Aveling and a Fowler, and these were tested during July and August of 1876 – some of the tests being witnessed by the Czar himself. Many different experiments were conducted, mainly of a military nature, and these took place on a variety of terrains, some of them extremely difficult and strewn with obstacles. It was found from this regime that the lighter, 8nhp Aveling was more satisfactory than the Fowler engine, which weighed 11 tons. The roads from Tsarskoe Selo to Ropscha and Kolpino were chosen for the long-distance trials, and a number of wooden bridges were to be negotiated; most of these crossings proved too light in construction to carry the weight of the Fowler engine and the versatility of the Aveling won the day. The carriage of baggage and freight was also undertaken, as was the hauling of artillery. By the time of the Russo-Turkish War of 1877, the

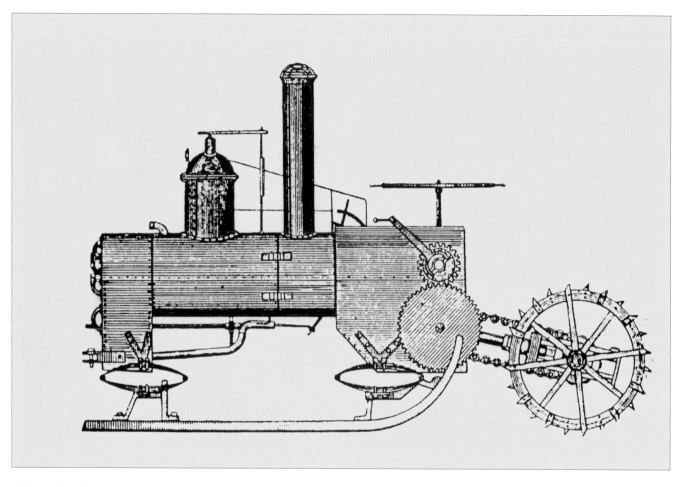

Fig. 3. Ice locomotive built on similar principles to the steam tractor opposite, manufactured by the inventor's son, P. Vradii. Also constructed in the 1860s.

Russians had seen the need for efficient transport in the field and selected the Aveling machine as a basis for meeting these needs. They also used a dozen engines based on that design in the conflict, with great success.

In the report by Maj. Viktor Demianiovich of the Russian Imperial Staff (Transport Dept.) that appeared in the *Russian Invalide* for 24th February 1879, an account of the work done by the traction engines was given – the Russian Government had ordered the 12 engines for military use just prior to the 1877 war and this proved to be a timely purchase; six units of the basic design were ordered from the British firm Aveling & Porter, of Rochester, Kent and these were the 8nhp type that had been tested in the summer of 1876. Four more were also ordered from Britain, from Messrs, Clayton & Shuttleworth of Lincoln. The remaining two machines were of domestic origin, from the Russian firm of Maltsev in Briansk.

These Maltsev engines exhibited many features common to both the Aveling and the Clayton machines, as may be noted from the illustration shown in Plate 1. The reason for this evident standardisation was that the purchase order had specified that the main parts of all of the engines must be interchangeable, and therefore it may be seen that the Maltsev had an Aveling style of boiler and motion, though it had a Clayton type of chimney; however, the Maltsev units were fitted with iron plate wheels of an indigenous form.

The Maltsev Zavod was an old established facility, having been founded by General Maltsev from Lyudinovo near Briansk in 1820. Originally the output of the company was restricted to general engineering products, but in 1870 the manufacture of steam railway locomotives commenced and between that date and 1881 some 373 such engines were constructed; also portable engines were made and, eventually, seven of the traction engines were completed for the Russian Imperial Army. These Maltsev engines were very successful, being in use for several years; they had a claimed output of 10nhp and were said to be able to haul loads of 19 tons behind them over very indifferent roads. The usage of the traction engines during the Russo-Turkish War of 1877-1878 was the first recorded application of mechanical

Fig. 4. Steam crawler tractor made by F. A. Blinov, allegedly in 1879.

that the Blinov engine proceeded in the direction of the 'shed' in front of the vertical boiler, and therefore it may be assumed that the stoker, and the necessary coals and water, were stored therein. The driver – who actually controlled the engine – sat in a comfortable seat at the rear, albeit in the cold; his left hand seems to be operating the track-laying mechanism, though the throttle and the reversing lever must also have been under his control. On the Vradii engines a separate drawn tender was used to carry coals and water, whilst the Maltsev engines were fitted with the normal, British style, integral tender.

Another track-laying vehicle was proposed by Vasiliy Dmitrievich Mendeleev (1886-1922) in the years prior to World War I. This gentleman was the son of the famous Russian scientist, and from 1903 until 1906 he was a pupil at the Kronstadt Marine Engineering College where he studied naval vessel design. From this college he went on to the St. Petersburg Shipyard where from 1908 to 1916 he was involved in the development of a powerful submarine engine of 1000bhp. Mendeleev had been interested in the production of armoured fighting vehicles, and he considered the submarine power unit suitable for propelling a large 'land-ship' or military tank. His original proposals called for a huge machine weighing 170 tons, with a large 120mm calibre naval gun mounted right at the front of the vehicle (Fig. 5). Armour plate thickness varied from 150mm at the front to 100mm on the sides, whilst the crew of 8 men made up the complement; other ideas were a form of pneumatic suspension for the track idler wheels, a four-speed and reverse gearbox, and a method of lowering the complete hull to protect the track-laying system. A servo arrangement operating by mechanical means through a gearbox and clutches made up the steering method; a small turret with machine guns was also incorporated in the specification.

Needless to say, the project was not fulfilled and the technical information and its allied drawings were archived in the collection of the Russian Academy of Science. Another similar project was instigated, replacing the main armament with a 127mm calibre naval gun, adding a second turret, and lowering weight by reducing the thickness of some of the armour to 50mm, but this scheme was also shelved by 1916. Other tracked vehicles were proposed and some of them actually produced during the early part of the 20th century; these are to be discussed in the chapter concerning Adolphe Kégresse.

Internal combustion engined tractors for agricultural use were also manufactured in the Czarist period, appearing between

transport under wartime conditions, and they effected a big saving over animal power, recovering their initial cost, and finally saving the Russian Government a sum of Ryb.6954.14, or over £80,000 at today's value.

In 1879 another form of steam tractor was made in Russia: the crawler engine shown in Fig. 4, built experimentally by F. A. Blinov. The tractor was driven by a horizontal steam engine installed on the right-hand side of the framing, which drove the third set of track wheels by means of spur gearing. Now, whilst the date claimed for this engine precedes the work in the USA of Alvin Lombard and Benjamin Holt, as well as the prototype made by the co-operation of Messrs Hornsby and Foster of Lincoln in England (which was constructed according to the patent specifications of David Roberts between 1899 and 1906), prior art does suggest that 1879 is a feasible date. In Russia itself, a specification for a track-laying and steam propelled engine was published by Captain Andreivich Zagriasky in 1837; also there had been a plethora of patent specifications for crawler and track-laying machines in the USA from the 1860s onwards. Coupled with the fact that the brilliant English inventor Sir George Cayley had revealed such a system in the 1820s, there appears to be no reason to doubt the Russian date.

Upon examination of the drawing in Fig. 4, it would seem

Fig. 5. The huge military tank projected by V. D. Mendeleev in the years before World War I, planned to weigh 170 tons and be fitted with a 120mm naval gun.

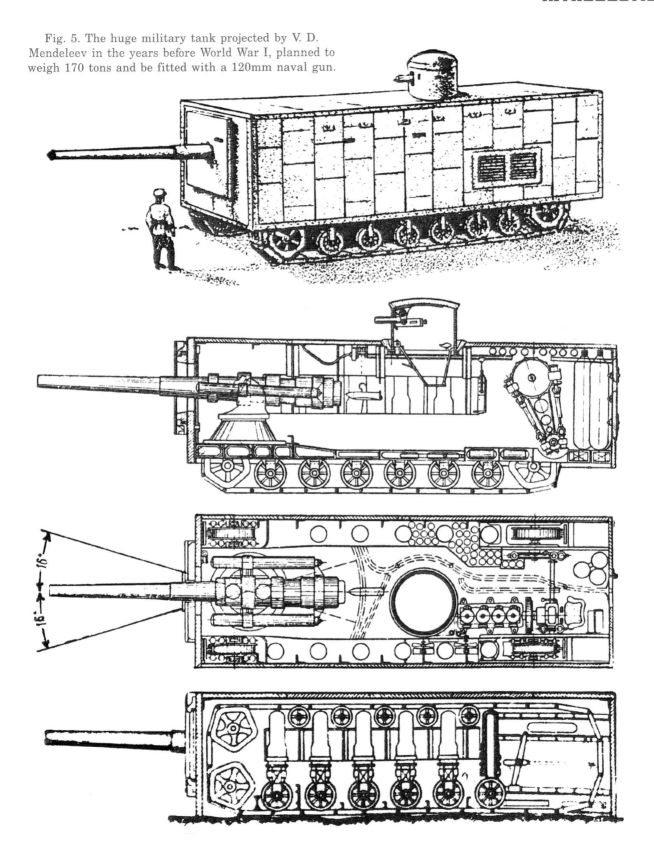

Fig. 6. The Russky tractor built by Ya V. Mamin.

Fig. 7. The Dwarf or Karlik three-wheeled tractor manufactured by Ya. V. Mamin just after World War I.

Fig. 8. The Yakovlev-Freze motorcar of 1896. The car is seen outside the pavilion of the 1896 All-Russia Industrial Exhibition at Nizhni-Novgorod.

1909 and the outbreak of World War I in 1914, emanating from a small firm named as the Ya. V. Mamina Zavod (Zavod means 'works'). Mamin managed to produce a large number of items during this time, including 180 threshing machines, 396 steam locomobiles, and about 10 wheeled tractors of a type named 'РУССКИ TRAKTOP' (Russky tractor); these latter machines were reminiscent of the Avery model from the USA (Fig. 6). Ya. Mamin managed to continue his work making tractors after 1917 when the then-new Soviet Government invited him to oversee a new plant entitled the Zavod Vozrozhdenie or 'Revival Factory', where he was allowed to develop further products, such as the small КАРЛИК, (Karlik, or 'Dwarf') – a three-wheeled, 12bhp tractor – and an experimental four-wheeler of 16bhp named 'ГНОМ' (Gnom, or 'Gnome'). Considerable numbers of the Karlik were supplied, but the Gnom remained as just a prototype.

Regarding passenger cars, the introduction of this form of personal transport came about when the first one was exhibited at the 1896 Industrial Exhibition in Nizhni Novgorod. This vehicle was the Yakovlev-Freze car, designed along Benz lines and with a 2bhp engine and belt drive; it was capable of about 13mph and it could be fitted with skis at the front to replace the wheels when snow was prevalent (Fig. 8).

Details of the various manufacturers of motorcars, trucks and buses made from the early 1900s to 1915 will be found in the following chapters, and these descriptions will commence with the most important make, the Russo-Baltiskii Vaggony Zavod in Riga, which is now in present day Latvia. The importation of chassis to be fitted with Russian built carriage-work is dealt with in Chapter 3.

Plate 1 (overleaf). Early vehicles made in the 19th & 20th centuries.

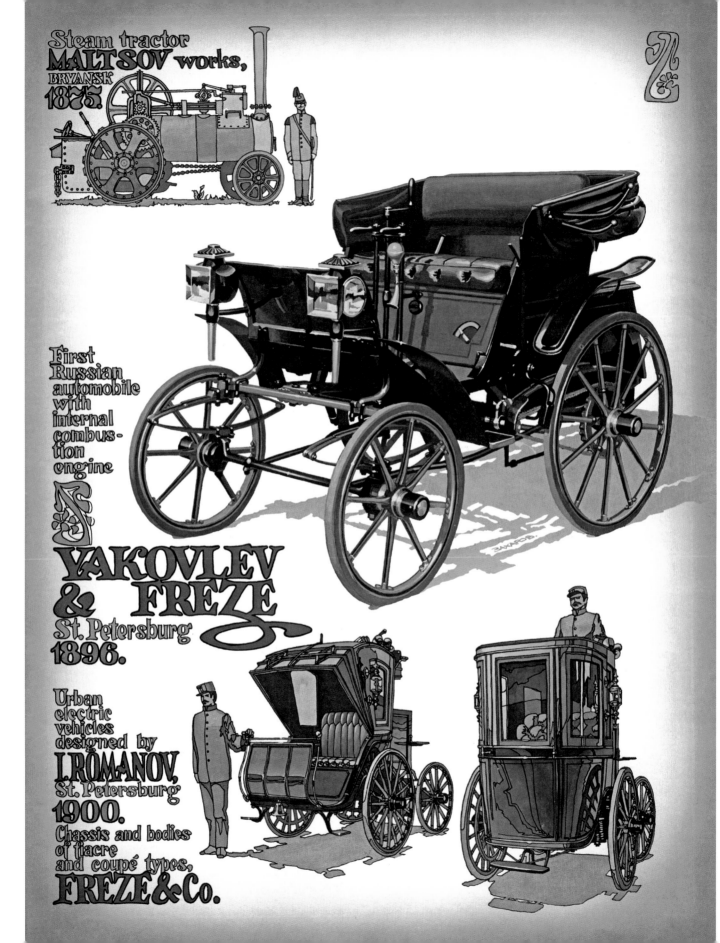

Steam tractor
MALTSOV works,
BRYANSK
1875.

First
Russian
automobile
with
internal
combus-
tion
engine

YAKOVLEV
& FREZE
St. Petersburg
1896.

Urban
electric
vehicles
designed by
I. ROMANOV,
St. Petersburg
1900.
Chassis and bodies
of fiacre
and coupé types,
FREZE & Co.

2. THE MANUFACTURERS

THE RUSSO—BALTISKII VAGONNYI ZAVOD, AUTOMOBILE DIVISION, RIGA, LATVIA

The Russo-Baltic Waggon Works at Riga in Latvia was by far the most successful of the pre-Revolutionary manufacturers within the old Russian Empire; it made a variety of other products besides automobiles, which included aircraft, railway equipment and wagons and heavy engineering items. It was renowned for the excellence of its products and was made famous by the introduction of the first four-engined aircraft to be built in series production in the world. Eighty of the giant

Ilya Muromets biplanes were made to the designs of the well known aeronautical engineer, Igor Sikorsky. The machine was so successful during the war that its very presence had a demoralising effect on the German forces, who were powerless to prevent it from penetrating their defences; in fact, only one Ilya Muromets was ever shot down by the enemy during the

Fig. 9. The first Russo-Baltique model S24/30 of 1909. This photograph is signed by Julian Potterat. (Courtesy N. Nemirovich, Polytechnical Museum of the USSR)

entire war, and in that action the Russian plane destroyed three of its assailants and severely damaged a fourth!

The automobile division of Russo-Baltic Waggon Works commenced operation in 1909, when Julian Potterat came from the obscure Belgian car manufacturer Automobiles Charles Fondu of Brussels and took up the position of Chief Engineer and Designer in the motorcar department of the Riga factory. He proceeded to design and produce the first Russo-Baltique car, known as the model S24/30 (series 1), completing it in May 1909 (Fig. 9). This car was a solidly designed machine, having a T-head, side-valve engine of 4.5-litre capacity, a three-speed sliding pinion gearbox, shaft drive, and a chassis of conventional layout; it was based upon the wares of Potterat's old firm in the city of Brussels. The illustration of the vehicle, dated 26th May 1909, is actually signed by the designer, and portrays the car fitted with a skimpy two seat roadster body. Anxious to demonstrate the capabilities of his new model, Potterat entered it for the Riga-St. Petersburg race on 30th May 1909, driving it himself in this reliability trial. The result was a very creditable time of 8 hours and 2 minutes for the 640km distance. The race

was advertised as being 600 versts in length; 'verst' being a Russian Imperial measure equal to 1.0668km.

Pleased with the car's showing in the May event, Potterat then entered it in the St. Petersburg-Riga-St. Petersburg contest in August 1909; this time he managed to achieve third place in the race, against stiff foreign competition in the shape of Mercedes and other leading European manufacturers – he completed the 1000 verst distance (1066.80km) in 16 hours and 7 minutes. These results confirmed that the Russians were quite capable of making motorcars that were able to compete on terms of equality with those made anywhere else, and, as will be shown later on in this narrative, were able to take on the pick of the classic marques and win quite comfortably! The writer considers that although the design of the vehicle was straightforward, even mundane, with its side-valve engine and three-speed gearbox, it was the care and precision with which the car was made and assembled that was the key to its success.

The S24/30-type continued in production for a couple of years until 1911, when it was superseded by an improved model designated the S24/35; this latter car was modified by

Fig. 10. Limousine-bodied S24/30 type Russo-Baltique of 1910. (Courtesy N. Nemirovich & Izdatelstvo Planeta)

Fig. 11. A line-up of Russo-Baltique K12/20 motorcars awaiting dispatch from the Riga factory in 1911.
(Courtesy N. Nemirovich, Polytechnical Museum of the USSR & Izdatelstvo Planeta Moskova)

uprating the engine to give a better horsepower output, and the name of the type signified the rating through the suffix digits 35. Apparently the original 30 model was continued into 7 series to cope with an order by the Russian Army, which evaluated it in a 320km test run held in May 1912. S24/30 models of series 1 to 3 were distinguished by level bonnets whilst the later series possessed sloping engine covers from 1912 onwards. Again in 1912, the basic design was uprated to 40bhp, and it was made at Riga in a variety of body styles, including enclosed limousines and landaulettes as the S24/40, which culminated in the series 18, built at Petrograd from July 1915 onwards.

The imminent arrival of the Kaiser's forces into Riga in 1915 forced the removal of the automobile division from the city, and it was evacuated to St. Petersburg, by then renamed Petrograd. Other departments also moved to Fili (a suburb of

Moscow), Tver (known today as Kalinin) and elsewhere. By September the Imperial German Army had occupied Riga, and the S24/40 model was built in the city of Petrograd from 1916 until 1919; however, truck production, which had been carried out since 1911, was terminated with the enforced move away from the Latvian capital. After the war the production of the Russo-Baltique was continued in Moscow when the factory at Fili was re-opened in August 1921 to manufacture the S24/40 which was then named as the Prombron, a Russian word meaning 'metal industry.' Manufacture continued until 1923 when the Soviet authorities terminated production.

Russo-Baltique cars were built for a period of 12 years in all, including the Soviet version, and they were popular with the upper echelons of Russian society, bought by courtiers to the Czar's court and top-ranking Government officials, and several examples were purchased by the Czar's Garage at Tsarskoe Selo near St. Petersburg. The vehicles were robust and well engineered with the designers always attempting to improve the models to provide better reliability and durability.

The S-series models showed several outward differences as the years went by, and these modifications are listed in this table:

Series numbers & modifications of the S-series Russo-Baltique motorcars			
Model	Series nos.	Year of manufacture	Modifications
S24/30	1 to 3	1909 – 1911	Flat bonnet line and flat topped mudguards.
S24/30	7	1911 – 1912	Sloping bonnet line and radiused mudguards.
S24/35	7	1912 onwards	Same as S24/30, series 7.
S24/35	12	1913	Higher sides to 'torpedo' style body, deeper windshield. Chassis frame strengthened with depth increased from 95mm to 120mm in the channel section. Increased wheelbase.
S24/40	14	1913	Revised radiator with water gauge in the header tank.
S24/40		1915	New rounded radiator shell, new type of rear axle. Wheelbase reduced to original dimensions.
S24/40	Prombron	1921 – 1923	Soviet version with increased radiator capacity, extended wheelbase and room for six passengers.

The general specifications of the S-types from the RVBZ for the original 1909 prototype are as follows: at first the car was fitted with a twin-block, T-head side valve power unit with a capacity of 4501cc and non-detachable heads. The engine had a compression ratio of 3.8:1 from 1909 until 1913, when it was increased to 4:1 and fitted with a new camshaft at the same time. In its final S24/40 form the engine could produce 40bhp at 1200rpm. Later on in 1913, covers were fitted to enclose the

Plate 2. Russo-Baltique passenger cars – S24/30 models (series 1 to series 18).

tappets and valve springs, the reciprocating oil pump was replaced by a gear driven one, and the sump oil capacity was increased.

All Russo-Baltic cars had bevel gear final drive, but before 1914 the axle casings were made of castings. However, these were modified by the use of stampings, and also the half shafts were manufactured from better material. The S24/30 and the S24/35 models had separate three-speed gearboxes, but with the introduction of the S24/40 model this item was replaced by a four-speed unit. The suspension was effected by semi-elliptic springing with a triple spring arrangement, with one spring-mounted transversely across the frame at the rear end in the manner of the Rolls-Royce or the French Delaunay-Belleville. The artillery type wheels had wooden spokes and they were fitted with 880 x 120mm, beaded-edge tyres; occasionally 880 x 135mm tyres were used. However, the early series 1 to 3 models were fitted with 880 x 105mm tyres.

The chassis frame was a stamping, and possessed a special sub-frame to support the engine; the depth of this stamping was increased from 95mm to 120mm in 1912. At the same time a new transmission brake was introduced, and the chassis fitted with redesigned brake and gear-shift levers. Radiators on the S24/35 model were enlarged, with an oval core and a water gauge glass in the header tank in 1913, but this style was discontinued in 1915 when a totally different type of radiator was installed on the S24/40 model.

With the provision of the new chassis frame the wheelbase was increased from 3165mm to 3305mm, but this was later reduced to its original size in 1915. Other minor changes were the provision of adjustable control pedals in 1913, and the replacement of the Russo-Baltic carburettor with a Zenith model 42 instrument on the S24/35 models. The S24/30 cars had a track of 1360mm, whilst the S24/35 had a measurement of 1375mm; the ground clearance of all models was 260mm, and the weight of the vehicle fitted with varying styles of coachwork ranged from 1820kg for the open 'torpedo' bodies to over 2000kg for enclosed, formal limousines. The rear axle loading was always kept to 56 per cent of the total vehicle mass.

Some modifications to the original specifications were made when production resumed at the Fill facility in Moscow after the war years; the new Prombron model had its engine power increased to 50bhp at 1600rpm, it had a standard open body giving an all up weight of 1750kg (dry), and had an increased wheelbase of 3200mm allowing accommodation for six seated passengers. Other improvements included a new design of water pump, increased radiator capacity with a redesigned shell, full electric lighting with DC generator, a modified gearbox and reduced axle height. The first example of the Prombron (ПРОМБРОНЬ) type left the factory on 8th October 1922, over a year after the re-opening of the plant, and it was numbered Chassis No. 1 again. The car was officially unveiled in Moscow by the Chairman of

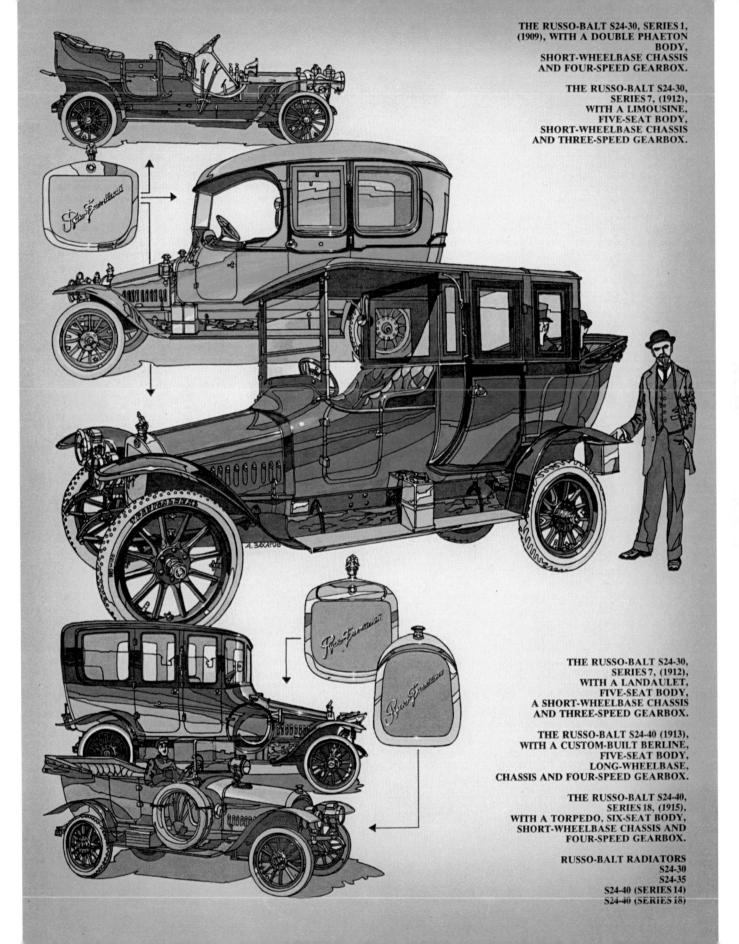

THE RUSSO-BALT S24-30, SERIES 1, (1909), WITH A DOUBLE PHAETON BODY, SHORT-WHEELBASE CHASSIS AND FOUR-SPEED GEARBOX.

THE RUSSO-BALT S24-30, SERIES 7, (1912), WITH A LIMOUSINE, FIVE-SEAT BODY, SHORT-WHEELBASE CHASSIS AND THREE-SPEED GEARBOX.

THE RUSSO-BALT S24-30, SERIES 7, (1912), WITH A LANDAULET, FIVE-SEAT BODY, A SHORT-WHEELBASE CHASSIS AND THREE-SPEED GEARBOX.

THE RUSSO-BALT S24-40 (1913), WITH A CUSTOM-BUILT BERLINE, FIVE-SEAT BODY, LONG-WHEELBASE, CHASSIS AND FOUR-SPEED GEARBOX.

THE RUSSO-BALT S24-40, SERIES 18, (1915), WITH A TORPEDO, SIX-SEAT BODY, SHORT-WHEELBASE CHASSIS AND FOUR-SPEED GEARBOX.

RUSSO-BALT RADIATORS
S24-30
S24-35
S24-40 (SERIES 14)
S24-40 (SERIES 18)

Fig. 12. The Russo-Baltique Stand No.1 at the 4th International Automobile Exhibition in St. Petersburg in 1913. (Courtesy N. Nemirovich)

Fig. 13. Andrei Platonovich Nagel & Vadim Alexandrivich Mikhailov seated in the Russo-Baltique 'Monako' car outside the Russian Imperial Automobile Club, prior to setting off in the Monte Carlo Rally on the morning of 13th January 1912; their wives are standing in front of the vehicle. (Courtesy N. Nemirovich, Polytechnical Museum of the USSR)

the All-Russian Central Executive Committee, M. I. Kalinin. This car is shown in Fig. 22.

Another range of passenger cars was introduced by the firm in 1910, and these were given the type identification nomenclature of K12. It would appear that these models were designed by a Dr Valentin who came from the German firm of Deutsche Automobil-Industrie, Hering und Richard AG in Ronneberg, which was the manufacturer of a car called the Rex-Simplex.

The K-series had a monobloc, L-head, side-valve engine that was originally rated at 15bhp at 1500rpm, with a capacity of 2211cc. This power unit was considerably more advanced in design than many contemporary engines, which were usually of the twin-block, T-head type, as used on the Russo-Baltique S-types. The K-type engine had four cylinders with bore and stroke measurements of 80 x 110mm. The crankcase and the three-speed gearbox casing were made of aluminium, whilst the final drive was by shaft. Thermo-syphon cooling, extensive use of ball bearings, exhaust gas pressure to raise the fuel to the carburettor, semi-elliptic springing at the front, and three-quarter elliptics at the rear completed the ensemble.

The wooden artillery wheels used on these cars were manufactured on special machinery installed at Riga, and this ensured a tight wheel that was produced in correct alignment, in contrast to the handmade wheels utilised by other firms. Use of nickel steel for the crankshaft, chrome/nickel and manganese/silicon steels for other parts of the car were all advanced technology at the time of manufacture. Russo-Baltic was also famed for the quality of its leaf springs, which were made by a special process, making them durable and long-lived; this was proved by the success of such springing on the firm's railway wagons, which never had to be replaced during the vehicles' lives.

Bodies fitted to the K-series cars included the ordinary 'torpedo' style, landaus, double-phaëtons and the French 'fiacre' style of coachwork. The original K12/15 was introduced at the 3rd International Motor Show at St. Petersburg, whilst an improved model entitled as the K12/24 which had an uprated engine of 24bhp was shown at the 4th International Motor Show in 1913. Three K-type models were exhibited at this latter venue: an open four seater, a rumble seat roadster, and a special two-seat speedster model. This latter model, shown in Plate 3, was designated the K12/30 Speedster, and had the engine bored out to 82mm, giving an increased capacity of 2322cc and a bhp figure of between 26 and 30 at 1400rpm.

In May 1911 it was recorded that I. Stephanov, a factory driver, achieved a standing start 1 verst run at a speed of 92kmh, this run believed to have been made in a K12 car; possibly the speedster shown at the 4th International Motor Show. Such cars were also used after the Revolution and War of Intervention in 1922 and 1923, and S. Viya is credited with a win in Class IV in the Petrograd-Pskov-Petrograd event in October 1922. Later on in June 1923, S. Kosyuk achieved a standing start speed of 104.65kmh on such a car. It is also on record that the factory driver, Ivanov, gained some successes in this postwar period,

though he possibly used an S-type car, perhaps chassis 610, which was an S24/40 model that appeared in the All-Russian Reliability Trials of 1923.

Luckily, one K12/15 torpedo bodied car has survived, and this vehicle was carefully restored to its former splendour by the staff of the Polytechnical Museum of the USSR in Moscow in 1966, and placed on show in the Motor Vehicle Gallery there. This example of the marque was manufactured in 1911 (Fig. 14). It is interesting to note that the name in script on the radiator core of this vehicle is in the Cyrillic form "РУССКО-БАЛТИСК," rather than the prevalent Russo-Baltique French style.

The Russo-Baltique car also made a name as a sporting machine quite quickly, as has been discussed in the previous paragraphs, and this was mainly due to the efforts of Andrei Platonovich Nagel, who was then a well-known Russian motoring sportsman and journalist. At first Nagel did not attach any importance to the make of car that he used, and a Brasier of French origin that he drove from St. Petersburg to Paris and back in the company of three friends suited him ideally. However, he attended the 3rd International Automobile Exhibition in the Michael Manege Hall in the capital in May 1910, and noticed the wares of the RVBZ displayed on stand Number 1, where several cars were exhibited. It used the slogan, "The first plant in Russia to build cars, using all its own services, including bodywork," and the show was a great success for it, as 20 units were sold from the stand.

Generally the exhibition was commercially successful; 50 cars in total were purchased that year, and as there were only 1056 motorcars in use in St. Petersburg at that time, this was considered an advance in car ownership. Nagel liked the style of the Russo-Baltique cars and ordered one there and then. In June 1910 he took delivery of a grey S24/30 model, 3rd series, Chassis No. 14. It had a rather large five-seat double-phaëton body, and Nagel first used it in competition in the Russian St. Petersburg-Kiev-Moscow-St. Petersburg Rally, with the well known French motoring journalist Charles Faroux as a passenger. The car performed very well, consuming fuel at a rate of 11 litres per 100km and averaging 83kmh on the journey. Faroux was amazed at its performance, but Nagel made light of it, claiming that the vehicle was quite ordinary with no sporting pretensions whatsoever; they finished in this rally without incurring any penalty points and received an award for their efforts. This was the first in a chain of rallies and events in which this car was to achieve success.

The next mention of Andrei Nagel and his Russo-Baltique Chassis No. 14 occurred when he had the idea of taking the car from Riga to Naples and then climbing to the site of the observatory on Mt Vesuvius! Accompanied by four companions, Nagel set off from St. Petersburg in August 1910. Leaving the Cathedral in Izaksky Square on a rainy morning, they set off for Riga, en route to Berlin, Prague, Nürnberg, Zurich, Turin, Genoa, Rome, and finally Naples. The Russian car aroused much interest in the various countries that they passed through, for it was an unusual sight to witness a Russian-built motorcar so far from home; the vehicle was also running on Russian made tyres, Provodnik-Riga (ПРОВОДНИК-РИГА), which were always used by Nagel. These tyres were one of the finest makes available anywhere prior to World War I, and were widely advertised in European and American motoring magazines where they were enthusiastically endorsed by sports correspondents and other journalists.

The run was reported in the German press, with the *Dresdener Anzeiger* newspaper giving a large amount of coverage to the event in its issue of 7th September 1910. Another interesting feature of this trip was that it was probably the first such run to be filmed, as one of the crew took a cine-camera with him and recorded the whole journey. In the following year, Nagel decided to participate in the St. Petersburg-Sevastopol Rally which covered a distance of 2240km. He also modified the car to make it suitable for long, high-speed runs, though this did increase the weight of the vehicle by 230kg. In a speed test prior to the Sevastopol run, the Russo-Baltique car managed to achieve a flying start average of 93kmh (57.66mph) over a distance of 1 verst. Together with the other 11 entrants in this rally, Nagel finished without penalty and was awarded a prize.

Andrei Nagel was to become the most famous and well known Russian sporting motorist before World War I. He was born on 2nd March 1877 and subsequently became a graduate of law at the Imperial St. Petersburg University; apart from his legal vocation, he was a member of the board, secretary and chairman of the Technical Commission of the Russian Imperial Automobile Society. He was also editor and publisher of a magazine entitled *The Automobile*, which was the official organ of the RIAS and was the first illustrated, technical motoring journal to be printed in Russia. The publishing office was at 36 Liteiny Prospekt St. Petersburg, which was in fact Nagel's home address. Whilst *The Automobile* was officially endorsed on its cover in English, French and German as being the RIAS house journal, it was eventually joined by two other technical publications prior to the outbreak of the 1914 war. These were *Air & Automobile Life* and *The Engine*, which were both edited and published by an engineer named Nikolai Gavrilovich Kuznetsov. Apart from the activities that Nagel was involved with and which are recounted above, he also became a sales agent for Russo-Baltique motorcars.

It was in 1912, however, that the name of Russo-Baltique burst upon the international competition scene with one of the most brilliant and epic drives ever recorded in rallying history – Andrei Nagel's drive from St. Petersburg to Monaco in the 1912 Monte Carlo Rally. This event was originally staged in a small way in 1911 and was a predominantly French inspired affair, but in 1912 it achieved full international status and competitors from many countries participated, starting out from assorted points in Europe, mainly capital cities, such as London and St. Petersburg. The latter venue was the furthest distance from the finish at Monte Carlo. As Andrei Nagel was intent on proving that his country could build and race a motorcar that was as good as any comparable vehicle produced elsewhere in the

world, he decided to enter one of the Russo-Baltique cars for this gruelling winter rally.

A special Russo-Baltique machine was entered for the Monte Carlo Rally, and the entry form for the event read as follows:

Type of car: Monako type S24/50 Torpedo Roadster
Driver: Andrei Platonovich Nagel
Co-driver: Vadim Alexandrovich Mikhailov

The Monako type of Russo-Baltique car was specially prepared with an uprated engine that developed 45bhp at 1500rpm and 50bhp at 1800rpm. This was achieved by increasing the stroke by 10mm to 140mm, which altered the capacity to nearly 5 litres (4939cc). The very elegant 'torpedo' type body that was fitted to this chassis was built under Nagel's supervision at the St. Petersburg branch of the Automobile Division of the Russo-Baltisky Vagonnyi Zavod at 10 Ertelev Street in the city. Other improvements made to the car included the fitting of aluminium pistons and a dual ignition system, and with these modifications, 60bhp could be produced for short bursts. The car is illustrated in Fig. 13 where it is shown outside the RIAS premises. In the driving seat is Andrei Nagel, who is accompanied by Mikhailov; their wives are standing beside the car prior to the epic run to Monte Carlo. Only the one example of the Monako type was ever produced by the RBVZ.

Preparations for the Rally were presumably carried out at 10 Ertelev Street and these include, again, the use of the Russian made tyres, Provodnik-Riga, which were expressly called for by Nagel. He also inserted another set of tyres within the 880 x 120mm covers that had the beads removed to give strength and support inside. Snow chains were fitted to the driving wheels, and acetylene lighting installed with a remote, running board-mounted generator, easily removed overnight as a precaution against frost, with a belt-driven DC dynamo driven off the engine as a standby, in case the gas lighting failed. The tyres were inflated to 75psi and a set of skis were to be attached to the steering wheels; these latter were deleted by Nagel just before the start, as he thought that they might prove more of a hindrance than a help in the packed snows he expected to encounter en route. A siren was mounted just behind the front right mudguard to 'deter bandits', whilst two ensign staffs were affixed to the dumb-irons to carry the Imperial Russian flags that were flown during the journey.

The Russo-Baltique S24/50 Monako, with Nagel driving and Mikhailov as passenger, set off from the Russian Imperial Automobile Club at 0800 hours on the morning of 13th January 1912, for the first leg from St. Petersburg to the overnight stop at Pskov. The weather conditions encountered on the first day were extremely cold (-22°C), and the competitors were beset with gusting winds, with deep snow causing the crew of the Russo-Baltique to dig themselves out on numerous occasions, with most of the running made in bottom gear. Later on, a severe blizzard occurred on the way to Riga, but the controls both there and at Königsberg were reached without any penalty. The roads from the latter checkpoint onwards had better conditions, and

Fig. 14. The restored Russo-Baltique K12/15 on exhibition in the Motor Vehicle Gallery of the Polytechnical Museum of the USSR. On the right of the car is a chassis of the ZIS-110 Limousine model from the immediate post-World War II period.

Berlin was made without any untoward incident. Good road conditions prevailed from here and Nagel was able to increase his speed through Germany, with the snow chains fitted to the rear wheels being discarded after Heidelberg had been passed. However, later on in France another set had to be procured because of bad ice on the hills.

The stops at Lyon and Avignon were made on time and Nagel and Mikhailov arrived in Monte Carlo on 23rd January, being the first competitors home, and therefore the outright winners! Nagel was forced to do all the driving in this fantastic run as his unfortunate co-pilot had fractured his wrist back in St. Petersburg when he was cranking the car to start it. Prince Louis of Monaco presented the Premier Prix des Itineraires, a Sèvres Vase and a specially commissioned sculpture to the intrepid winners, and this Russian car with its Russian team had become the first car to win an International Monte Carlo Rally. They had covered the longest distance in the rally, against competition from the cream of Europe's manufacturers and drivers.

In the summer of 1912, Andrei Nagel set off once again on another marathon event, Moscow to San Sebastian via St. Petersburg. This long distance attempt by Nagel was the second international event that Russo-Baltic was involved in during 1912, and he used the faithful Chassis No. 14 again for the run. Just prior to the Spanish trip, this car had undergone a special body change adapting it for long-distance runs – spares, tools, extra lubricants and fuel were stowed in compartments on the running boards and in the wings. A new body was manufactured at 10 Ertelev Street, the HQ of the RBVZ in St. Petersburg, which was of the 'four-seater torpedo' type; it had everything needed at that time for the lengthy event, viz., enlarged header tank for the radiator, two extra large fuel tanks containing sufficient fuel for a journey of 530km without stops, and specially designed seating for comfort.

Initially, the re-bodied car made a trial run from St. Petersburg to Moscow, via Grodno and Smolensk, to return to the capital – a distance of 3000km. This run was completed

Russo-Balt of the 1913 K12-24 model
with a landau four-seat body.
The engine's displacement volume
was 2,211 cc.
It had 4 cylinders, 24 hp
and could travel at 65 kph.

Russo-Balt K12-24 sporting
two-seater of 1912.
Its displacement volume was 2,322 cc.
The engine had 4 cylinders,
26 to 30 hp and could
develop 105 kph.

Plate 3. Russo-Baltique passenger cars – K12/24 models.

without any involuntary stops or other failures, and Nagel considered the vehicle fit to compete in the gruelling Moscow-San Sebastian event. The Russo-Baltique, Chassis No. 14, driven by A Nagel, set off from Moscow in August 1912 and it covered the trip of 4492km without any untoward circumstances. For this effort, car and driver took 3rd place overall in a field of 104 competitors.

By the beginning of 1913, Chassis No. 14 had covered a distance of 52,000km, which was an exceptional amount for that time. However, not satisfied with his previous exploits, Nagel set out once more with Chassis No. 14 on a protracted tour of towns and cities in Central Russia, the Volga Region, Byelorussia and the Ukraine, coming back to St. Petersburg via Riga, the home of the Russo-Baltic factory. This journey added another 11,000km to the total traversed by the car, and one of the travellers who accompanied Nagel on the run wrote in his diary "... in general, our car has given excellent service so far – not a single failure. The tyres are also very good; we have St. Petersburg's air in the front inner tubes and hope to carry it back to St. Petersburg."

Later on in the autumn of 1913, Nagel undertook a trip to Africa. Chassis No. 14 was used once more and the vehicle was carefully checked out prior to the journey; two electric lamps were fitted to augment the existing acetylene headlights, and a powerful horn was installed, all powered by an auxiliary generator. The artillery wheels, which were heavy, and therefore strong, were covered with aluminium disks to prevent mud clogging in between the spokes, whilst a leathern apron was placed beneath the radiator to reduce mud and splashes contaminating the bodywork and the underside of the car.

Travelling in company with two of the staff from his journal, Nagal's itinerary was made as follows – from St. Petersburg they were to proceed through Germany, France and Spain to cross the Mediterranean to Morocco, and thence through Algeria and Tunisia, crossing back across the sea to Italy and on to Paris, where they would be met by the redoubtable Charles Faroux. This excursion covered a distance of 13,000km, and in Africa the group entered the Sahara Desert, arrived at Biskra Oasis and climbed the Atlas Mountains to a height of 1300 metres above sea level. As a result all of these escapades, Nagel and his Russo-Baltique, Chassis No. 14 had travelled some 80,000km in four years without any major repairs, and with the Provodnik tyres giving excellent results. Charles Faroux, the editor of the French motoring journal *L'Auto*, who had previously accompanied Nagel on the St. Petersburg-Kiev-Moscow run in 1910 (see page 23) thought the performance of the Russian car was beyond reason, with the exclamation "C'est impossible!"

Another prominent Russian driver in the pre-World War I era was Ivan Ivanov, who was a mechanic at the St. Petersburg branch of the Russo-Baltic concern. He had a Russo-Baltique S24/55 model converted into a racing car by Engineer Ivan

Friazinovsky. Presumably, this conversion was also carried out at 10 Ertelev Street, and it was effected by replacing the touring-phaëton body with streamlined, cigar-shaped carriage-work, replacing the artillery wheels with lighter Rudge-Whitworth centre-lock wire wheels fitted with Provodnik 880 x 120mm competition tyres, and increasing the power output from 55bhp to 58bhp. The axle ratio was also lowered in a bid to improve the maximum speed of the car. This car was dubbed the 'Russky Ogurets' (РУССКИ ОГУРЕЦ), or 'Russian Cucumber,' due to its cigar shape and green colouring. Using this car Ivanov set an all-Russian record for domestically produced automobiles on 27th May 1913. He covered the flying verst (1068 metres) at an average speed of 130kmh, or approximately 80mph. This feat won a prize of a special cut-glass bowl, which was made specifically for the event.

A week later, at the 1913 Grand Prix de Ste. Petersbourg, Ivanov appeared again, driving the S24/58 'Cucumber' against notable European competition. Entries from many other countries were accepted for the race, including Renef Notombes of Belgium driving an Excelsior, the Swiss car designer Marc Birkgigt driving his Hispano-Suiza, Luigi Rietti of Italy, Arthur Duray of France, and so on. Other important cars appearing were the German Benz, 29/60 Prince Henry model and the Belgian Metallurgique. The course comprised 7 laps making up a total of 276km. The Russian car achieved 2nd place, leaving Notombes, Birkigt and Duray behind!

For the 1914 season the car was redesigned, with a new style of single-seater body, a long pointed tail, a 'wind cutting' radiator shell, and an improved engine of 5033cc capacity that was able to produce 60bhp. This car was designated the S24/60, and it was again entered for the 1914 Grand Prix de Ste Petersbourg with Ivan Ivanov driving. Unfortunately, technical troubles dogged the car this time out and the vehicle did not complete the course. The outbreak of World War I terminated motor racing in Europe, and the racing Russo-Baltique vehicle disappeared without a trace; it was probably destroyed during the hostilities that ensued with Russia's entry into the fray. Both versions of this racing car are illustrated in Plate 6.

Some other types of Russo-Baltique passenger cars were also manufactured by the Riga plant, and these differed in design from the two main streams of the company's output. There was the massive 40/60 model of 1911/1912, which was a great 7.2-litre monster that stood on a wheelbase of 11 foot and was fitted with a larger version of the T-head, S-series power unit. Unfortunately, the writer has been unable to discover an illustration of this vehicle. An unusual motorcar was built for the 1914 season, designated the E-15/35 model, which sported an elliptical radiator shell, distinguishing it from all other Russo-Baltique models. This car was supplied with an L-head, monobloc engine of 3684cc capacity that produced 35bhp at 1500rpm. Due to the onset of war in 1914, the E-type was withdrawn in 1915. Some taxis and formal limousines designated the D-24/40 were also built on a van chassis just prior to the war.

The 1912 Russo-Balt-S24-35
(4,501 cc, 35 hp),
featuring a double-phaeton
five-seat body on a chassis with
a 3,160-mm wheelbase.

The 1913 Russo-Balt-K12-20
(2,211 cc, 20 hp),
featuring a limousine four-seat
body on
a chassis with a 2,850-mm
wheelbase.

The 1914 Russo-Balt-D24-40
(4,501 cc, 40 hp),
featuring a landaulet
six-seat body on a chassis
with a 3,375-mm wheelbase.

The 1915 Russo-Balt-E15-35
(3,684 cc, 35 hp),
featuring a torpedo
five-seat body on a chassis
with a 3,250-mm
wheelbase.

Plate 4. Russo-Baltique passenger cars – various D, E, K and S models.

In the 1990s the staff of the Polytechnical Museum in Moscow discovered a small experimental car of 1912 from the Russo-Baltic factory's archive material; this was given the nomenclature 8/12. It was probably a pilot prototype for a smaller range, and was fitted with a four-cylinder power unit of 1311cc capacity. (The E-15/35 is depicted in Plate 4).

RUSSO-BALTIC BUS & TRUCK MODELS

Apart from the passenger cars previously described, a considerable number of commercial vehicles were also produced by the firm. The Russian truck market in the first years of the 20th century was dominated by foreign manufacturers, mostly German. A Russian technician, Boris Lutsky, had worked for the Daimler firm on the design staff, and he had some hand in the design of the Daimler-Marienfelde 5-ton truck, of which two were exported into Russia during 1901; he went on to become a leading figure on the design branch of the GA Lessner company, an enterprise that was to be prominent in the early days of the Russian motor industry. Although the commercial vehicle market in Russia was the province of foreigners, Russo-Baltic decided to enter it in order to provide Russian enterprises with Russian-made vehicles. To this end two models were made from 1911 onwards, the D-25/35 already mentioned, and the M-24/35 with a 2/3-ton payload. These two were later joined by a larger 5/6-ton truck designated the T-40/65.

The first series of truck models to be produced by the Russo-Baltic Waggon Works was the M-type, which came out in 1911 (Fig. 18). It had the standard 35hp, 4501cc car engine installed, and it could be fitted with a number of differing bodies, including flat platform, sided truck, bulk liquid tanker and sometimes omnibus carriage-work. The M-type had a four-speed, sliding pinion 'crash' gearbox, with a final drive by countershaft that incorporated the differential, and pitch-chains that drove chainwheels attached to each rear wheel, the axle being 'dead.' Its wheelbase was 3400mm, its weight at the kerb 1920kg, and its top speed was a mere 20kmh. Its rated payload was between 2 and 3 tons.

The other model that appeared in 1912 was the D-24/35, which was initially designed and produced as a van; in this guise it served as a mail van for the Russian post office, and it was also employed as an ambulance. These trucks were also fitted with the 35hp car engine of 4501cc capacity, but had a payload of only 1 ton, which made them more speedy on the road, being capable of 40kmh. The wheelbase was 3375mm, the kerb weight 1600kg, and a 4-speed gearbox was linked to shaft drive. Soon after its introduction other body styles were added to the range, and sometimes formal limousines were ordered on the D chassis (Plate 4). Wagonettes and sided truck bodies were fitted, and interestingly, the chassis was occasionally utilised to give service as a fire-fighting appliance; a fire engine of this type was exhibited at the 4th International Automobile Exhibition

in St. Petersburg in 1913, along with nine other models from the firm. One of the two Russo-Baltic vehicles known to have survived today is a model D fire engine (Plate 7).

Some parts of a vehicle known to have been supplied to the Peter's Fire-Fighting Union of Riga in 1912 were discovered circa 1979 by members of the Vintage Car Club of Riga, cemented into the base of a radio aerial mast in the city, and forming part thereof. These parts included the chassis frame, the steering column, and sundry gearbox and transmission components. The location of this find was actually in Rauna, in the Valmiera District, which is just outside Riga itself. It took 18 months to retrieve and restore the vehicle, using some parts from four different vehicles together with new items, eventually allowing the club to present it in a working condition. The only concession to modernity was the use of GAZ truck rims, as pre-1930 tyres were unobtainable in the Soviet Union at that time. Today, the fire engine is the centre-piece of an exhibition in the Riga Museum of Fire-Fighting Equipment.

The final Russo-Baltic truck model, the T-40/65, entered service again in 1912. This vehicle was a much larger unit than the other commercial vehicles in the company's range, and it was a rugged, solid machine ideally suited for Russian conditions. The vehicle had a payload of 5 or 6 tons, and was supplied with a large four-cylinder, 7850cc petrol engine, which was probably of the T-head, twin-block, variety. It had a four-speed, sliding pinion gearbox with final drive from a countershaft/differential to sprockets, pitch-chains, and chainwheels on the rear road wheels. These road wheels were of the wooden, artillery type, of very robust construction; they were fitted with solid rubber tyres and the diameter of the rear ones was 1.03 metres, or nearly 3ft 6in. The engine could produce 65bhp at 800rpm and it was fitted with two spark plugs per cylinder to cope with the dual ignition; the gearbox was fitted with ball bearings throughout. The dual ignition system incorporated both magneto and battery and coil, and it had an automatic advance and retard mechanism (very modern for the time). Aluminium castings were used for both the crankcase and gearbox casing.

Braking was applied in three ways: firstly, on the gearbox (probably by an external contracting drum fitted to the back of the gearbox); secondly, on the differential (probably as a differential lock); and thirdly, on drums attached to the rear wheels. It is not clear how the braking was actually operated, but at that time it was common practice for the foot-brake to control the transmission drum, the handbrake the rear wheel drums and the differential lock to be applied by hand underneath the vehicle.

Examples of these models were pressed into use by the Russian Army during World War I, with the D-type being the most prolific; not so many M and T-types were in service, but the latter model was the first to have anti-aircraft guns mounted on it.

In five years of production the Russo-Baltic Waggon Works produced over 299 commercial vehicles, but as with the passenger cars only one has survived. Car production is noted in a separate table appended to this chapter.

Fig. 15. A wagonette/shooting break style of body fitted to a Russo-Baltique model D24/35 chassis.

All Russo-Baltic motor vehicles were almost entirely manufactured within the company factory, with very few items being bought out. Most of the units such as radiators, lamps, acetylene generators and wheels were made in the various departments of the RBVZ, though tyres were purchased from either Tbo. Provodnik-Riga or Treugolnik-St. Petersburg in Russia, or Continental in Germany. Also, the factory possessed special machinery for making artillery wheels, which ensured that the components, the felloes, the spokes etc., were machined with greater precision than hand work would have achieved; this allowed better alignment and truth together with better fitting joints.

Some lamps were obtained from the French firm Franconia, whilst magnetos and other electrical equipment came from Robert Bosch GmbH, as did the sparkplugs. Some Russo-Baltic vehicles had Magneto Système Potterat fitted; magnetos were also made at the Singer Sewing Machine Works in Podolsk during the period under review.

Apart from civilian vehicles, the Russo-Baltic Waggon Works is known to have built a number of armoured cars for the Russian Army in the immediate prewar years (Fig. 21). The first of these military vehicles appeared in 1913, whilst several more were manufactured right up to the outbreak of hostilities in 1914. They were destined for the newly formed Russian Army Automobile Corps; this regiment had a number of assorted vehicles both foreign and domestic, and several of them were either armoured by local engineering works such as the Putilov Zavod in St. Petersburg or the Idzhorski Zavod, or just armed as has been noted with the Russo-Baltic T-type with anti-aircraft guns. These Russo-Baltic armoured cars were fitted with dual controls in order that another crew member could take control if the driver was incapacitated; a further set of controls was installed at the rear of the hull for the same reason.

In all, the products of the Russo-Baltic Waggon Works were of excellent quality, well in line with the best made by foreign manufacturers; that the company would have gone on to better things is indisputable had not World War I and the subsequent Bolshevik Revolution intervened. Other motor

Plate 5. Sporting versions of the Russo-Baltique S24/30 model.

A Russo-Balt of the S24-30 model, third series, of 1910
(chassis No. 14)
with a five-seat double phaeton body.

The chassis of the
Russo-Balt-S24-30, 1910.
The wheel base is 3,156 mm,
the weight of the body is 1,168 kg,
and the size of the tires is
880×120 mm.

The four-seat Grand Tourismo
body,
1912 on the Russo-Balt-S24-30
chassis No. 14.

The Russo-Balt was equipped
with two additional electric lamps
for its trip around
Africa in 1913.

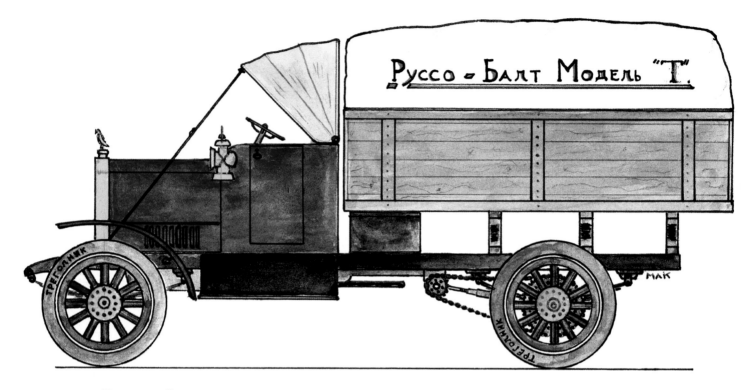

РУССО - БАЛТ МОДЕЛЬ "Т".

RUSSO-BALTIQUE MODEL "T" 5-ton TRUCK 1913~1914.

Fig. 16. Side elevation drawing of the Russo-Baltique T40/65 5/6-ton truck model.

manufacturers in Czarist Russia such as Lessner and Puzyrev also made quality vehicles, whilst Russian coachbuilders were amongst the best in the world at that time. Despite the fact that the Czarist authorities did not actively encourage industrial production, and that other countries believed "Russians will never be good engineers," there were many facilities that could make a variety of items of as good quality as anywhere else; such organisations as the Putilov Zavod, the Nikolai Shipyard in St. Petersburg, the Kolumna Locomotive Works, and so on, all made first-class industrial products.

To conclude the saga of the Russo-Baltic Waggon Works – a testimonial from a 'satisfied user' sent to the Russian journal *Avtomobil* in the September of 1910. A. Mamontov, the director of a large engineering firm in Briansk (possibly the Maltsev Zavod), told of his experience with his 24/30 model in the following words: "... In the interests of the development of the Russian motor industry I deem it my duty to tell you about a trip in my car manufactured by the Russo-Balt Railway Car Works ... I am delighted with the car ... the vehicle behaved beyond reproach during the whole journey;

not a single breakdown or fault. The body workmanship is good. The springs are excellent. I am under the impression that the vehicles made by the Russo-Balt Works are in no way inferior in their qualities to those of the best motor works in other countries."

NOTE: Those crew members who accompanied A. P. Nagel on the Africa Run in Chassis No. 14 were as follows:

Boris Nikiforov: A correspondent of *The Automobile* who had toured the United States reporting on the motor industry there under the pen-name of 'Bob Wilson from New York,' and who collaborated with reports concerning the Africa expedition with articles entitled *In Pursuit Of The Sun*.

Evgeny Kuzmin: Another correspondent from *The Automobile*. Nagel and his companions were all members of the Russian Imperial Automobile Society.

Plate 6. Racing versions of Russo-Baltique cars – S24/55 Monako, S24/58 Russky Ogurets, and the S24/60 Grand Prix model.

RUSSO-BALT S24-58, 1913, RUSSIA'S RECORD HOLDER.
ENGINE: 4 CYLINDERS, T-SHAPED VALVE ARRANGEMENT, DISPLACEMENT—4,939 cc, RATING—58 hp AT 1,800 rpm. WEIGHT OF CAR ABOUT 1,280 kg. TOP SPEED—130 kph.

RUSSO-BALT S24-55, 1911, FOR MONTE-CARLO RALLY.
ENGINE: 4 CYLINDERS, T-SHAPED VALVE ARRANGEMENT, DISPLACEMENT—4,939 cc, RATING—55 hp AT 1,800 rpm. WEIGHT OF CAR ABOUT 1,500 kg. TOP SPEED—113 kph.

RUSSO-BALT S24-60, 1914, FOR ST. PETERSBURG GRAND PRIX RACES.
ENGINE: 4 CYLINDERS, T-SHAPED VALVE ARRANGEMENT, DISPLACEMENT—5,033 cc, RATING—60 hp AT 1,800 rpm. WEIGHT OF CAR ABOUT 1,300 kg. TOP SPEED—130 kph.

Fig. 17. The power unit for the Russo-Baltic S24/30 passenger car, series 1 to 7. (Courtesy N. Nemirovich)

Fig. 18. The Russo-Baltic type-M 2-ton truck of 1914. (Courtesy V/O Avtoexport)

RUSSO-BALT-M TRUCK.
1914.
CARRYING CAPACITY 2 TONS.
KERB WEIGHT 1.9 TONS.
FOUR-CYLINDER, 40 hp ENGINE.
SPEED 20 kph.

Fig. 19. Views inside the Russo-Baltic factory, showing completed chassis (left) ready for transfer to the body shop. (Courtesy N. Nemirovich)

Fig. 20. Advertisement for Russo-Baltic Motor Cars (see right for translatory note).

Limited Company
Russo-Baltic Waggon Factory
@ Riga

Office: St. Petersburg, Gogol Street, House No. 13
Telephone nos: 2-74, 506-18, 568-24

RUSSIAN AUTOMOBILES

Special construction for Russian roads

With new style carriagework

St. Petersburg Works Department
Russo-Baltic Waggon Factory
Ertelev 10,
Telephone: 469-07

REPRESENTATION

@ KIEV Engineer V. B. Popelskii,   @ ODESSA
   Alexandrosaya no. 47
@ EUPATORIA I. M. Kefeli &   @ ROSTOV-ON-DON
   S. E. Duvan (Crimea)
@ EKATERINODAR & BAKU   @ KHARKOV
   Top floor, Stkek & Co.

Top floor, "Engineer
Brdzhostovich
Karnitskii
Zakrzhevskii"
Kharvov, Suiskaya
no. 1

Fig. 21. The Russo-Baltic armoured car, designed in 1913 with production commencing in 1914. They were probably based on the D-type chassis, using the S-24/40 engine. The vehicles seemed to have been assembled at 10 Ertelev St in St. Petersburg and were armoured at the Izhorski Zavod in Kolpino. The armour plate had a thickness of between 4 and 12mm, and the car was armed with three Maxim machine guns. Altogether, some sources state that 120 units were manufactured from 1914 until 1918 – this output figure does enhance the known production figures for the Russo-Baltic factory.

Fig. 22. The Soviet version of the S-24/40, the Prombron. Engine uprated to 45hp (33kw) at 1800rpm. Length – 5040mm. Width – 1600mm. Wheelbase – 3200mm. Wheel diameter – 1365mm. Weight all up – 1850kg. Maximum speed 75kmh.

MODEL CHART
1) PASSENGER CARS

Date	Model	Mechanical details	Tyres	Dimensions	Payload	Max. speed
1909-12 Series: 1 to 7	S24/30	Engine: 4501cc twin-block, 105 x 130mm bore and stroke. 30bhp at 1200rpm. Transmission: 3-speed, final drive by shaft.	880 x 120mm	Wheelbase: 3160mm. Weight: 1820kg.	5/6 seat	75kmh
1911-12 Series: 8 to 12	S24/35	Engine & transmission: As for above model, except 35bhp at 1200rpm.	All other details same as above model.			
1913-15	S24/40 (Riga)	Engine: As for the above models but 40bhp at 1200rpm. Transmission: 4-speed, final drive by shaft.	880 x 120mm	Wheelbase: 3305mm. Weight: 1850kg.	5/6 seat	80kmh
1916-19 Series: to 18	S24/40 (Petrograd)	Identical to the Riga type.	880 x 120mm	Wheelbase: 3165mm. Weight: 1840kg.	5/6 seat	80kmh
1911	S24/50	Monako Sports Roadster type. Engine: As for 30hp type but stroke extended to 140mm. 45bhp at 1500rpm and 50bhp at 1800rpm. 4939cc. Transmission: 4-speed with final drive by shaft.	880 x 120mm	Wheelbase: 3305mm. Weight: Not stated.	2 seats	80kmh

Date	Model	Mechanical details	Tyres	Dimensions	Payload	Max. speed
1913	S24/60	Russky-Ogurets racing model. As for 30bhp model by 107 x 140mm bore and stroke. 60bhp at 5033cc. Transmission: 4-speed final drive by shaft.	–	Wheelbase: 3305mm. Weight: Not stated.	2 seats	130kmh
1910	K12/15	Engine: 2211cc monobloc, bore & stroke 80 x110mm. 15bhp at 1500rpm. Transmission: 3-speed with final drive by shaft.	810 x 100mm	Wheelbase: 2855mm. Weight: Not stated.	4 seats	60kmh
1911-12	K12/20	Engine: As for the previous model except rating – 20bhp at 1500rpm. Transmission: 3-speed with final drive by shaft	810 x 100mm	All other details same as the previous types.		
1913-15	K12/24	Engine: As for the K12/15 except for rating of 24bhp at 1600rpm. Transmission: 3-speed with final drive by shaft.	810 x 100mm	Wheelbase: 2655mm. Weight: 1180kg. Grnd. Clr. – 220mm. Fuel cons. – 17l/100km.	4 seats	70kmh
1911-13	K12/30	Sports model. Engine: As for the K12/15 but increased capacity to 2422cc. 40bhp at 1400rpm. Transmission: 3-speed with final drive by shaft.	–	Wheelbase: 2655mm. Weight: Not stated.	2 seats	95kmh
1914-15	E15/35	Engine: 3684cc L-head, monobloc 95 x 135mm bore & stroke, 35bhp at 1500rpm. Transmission: 4-speed with final drive by shaft.	880 x 130mm	Wheelbase: 3250mm. Weight: 1500kg.	4/5 seat	75kmh
1911-12	40/60	Limousine. Engine: 7235cc. T-head, twin-block with 120 x 160mm bore & stroke. 4-cylinder with 60bhp at 1500rpm. Transmission: 4-speed with final drive by shaft.	935 x 135mm	Wheelbase: 3480mm. Weight: According to coachwork.	7/8 seat	100kmh
1912	8/12	Engine: 4-cylinder. 1311cc.	Other details not recorded. Was pilot experimental vehicle for proposed light car range.			

2) COMMERCIAL VEHICLES

Date	Model	Mechanical details	Tyres	Dimensions	Payload	Max. speed
1912-15	D	Engine: 24/40 or 24/35. Transmission: 4-speed with final drive by shaft.	Solid front & pneumatic rear.	Wheelbase: 3375mm. Weight: 1600kg.	1 ton	40kmh
1913-15	M	Engine: 24/35 and 24/40. Transmission: 4 -speed with final drive by chain.	Solid.	Wheelbase: 3400mm. Weight: 1920kg.	2 tons	20kmh
1913	MO	Omnibus model. Engine: 24/40. Transmission: 4-speed with final drive by chain.	Solids or pneumatic.	Wheelbase: 3760mm.	12 seats	20kmh
1913-15	T 40/60	Heavy truck. Engine: 7850cc twin-block, T-head. 65bhp at 800rpm. Transmission: 4-speed with final drive by chain.	Solids.	Wheelbase: 3650mm. Weight: 4220kg.	5/6 tons	20kmh

Notes on Russo-Baltic models	
S24/30	Series 1 current 1909. Series 2 current 1909-1910. Series 3 current 1910-1911. Series 4, 5 & 6 current from 1911-1912. Series 7 current 1912 (army staff).
S24/35	Series 8 to 12 current from 1911-1912.
S24/40	Series 14 commenced at Riga and finished at Series 18 in Petrograd.
Prombron	Model built 1922-1923.

PRODUCTION FIGURES

These production figures were given in A. S. Isaev's book, and may only be construed as a guide to annual output.

All types:	1909 – 10 units. 1910 – 10 units. 1911 – 33 units. 1912 – 78 units. 1913 – 100 units. 1914 – 140 units. 1915 – 90 units.

Note: Research in the Polytechnical Museum confirmed that altogether 1200 units of both passenger cars and commercial vehicles were made from 1909 to 1919. A late prewar Chassis No. 610, which was a model 24/40, was involved in the All-Russian Reliability Trials of 1923. As only 461 units are accounted for in the above list, No. 610 must have been made during World War I. Probably the balance from 1915 to 1919 were vehicles built for the war effort.

ADDRESSES OF THE DIVISIONS OF THE RBVZ
1) Head office: 13 Gogol Street, St. Petersburg. (Tel: 2-74, 508-18 & 568-24)
2) Workshops: 10 Ertelev Street, St. Petersburg. (Tel: 469-07)
3) Factory: RBVZ, Automobile Division. Riga, Latvia.

EXHIBITIONS WHERE RUSSO-BALTIC VEHICLES WERE DEMONSTRATED
1) The 2nd international motor Exhibition, St. Petersburg – 1910.
2) Aeronautical Exhibition, St. Petersburg – 1911.
3) The Czar's Royal Jubilee Exhibition – 1911.
4) The 4th international motor Exhibition – 1913.

EXHIBITION & SPORTING AWARDS GIVEN TO RUSSO-BALTIC VEHICLES
1) Large gold medals gained at the 2nd and 4th International Motor Exhibitions and at the Czar's Royal Jubilee Exhibition.
2) St. Petersburg-Riga-St. Petersburg Race – 3rd place – August 1909.
3) Monte Carlo Rally – 1st place overall – Premier Prix des Itineraires for the longest distance covered. Also the Sèvres Vase and the Volton Sculpture – January 1912.
4) Moscow-San Sebastian Rally – 2nd place overall. Special Gold Cup Award for longest distance travelled – August 1912.
5) Circumnavigation of the Mediterranean – 15,000km traversed. Awarded the Great Gold Medal of the War Ministry – 1913.

NB: Another large gold medal was awarded to the RBVZ at the 1911 Aeronautical Exhibition for the 4-engined Illyia Muromets aircraft, the first such aeroplane to be constructed in the world.

Plate 7. The surviving Russo-Baltique model D fire appliance.

BIBLIOGRAPHY

Books:

Automobilia Vestures Lappuses (History of the Automobile) – E. Lipins, Zinatne Riga – 1983 (Latvian text).

Avtomobil Strana Sovetov (Soviet Automobiles) – L. M. Shugurov & V. P. Shirshov, Isdatelstvo Dosaaf, Moscow – 1980 (Russian text).

Ot Samobegloii Kolyaski Do Zil-111 (Early Days to Zil-111) – A. S. Isaev, Isdatelstvo Moskobskii Rabochii, Moscow – 1961 (Russian text).

Tanki (Tanks) – Col. V. D. Mostovenko, Isdatelstvo veonizdat, Moscow – 1958 (Russian text).

Journals:

Automobile Quarterly no. 2 – Alec Ullman, 1976.

Automobile Revue (Swiss journal)– December 1974 – Item concerning Nagel and Moscow-San Sebastian run (German text).

Dresdener Anzeiger (German newspaper) – 7th September 1910 – account of the Naples run.

ACKNOWLEDGEMENT

To Nikolai Nemerovich, the Reference Director at the former Polytechnical Museum of the USSR for information used in this text and for reading and correcting the manuscript. Also for supplying original photographs for use in the narrative.

Plate 8 (overleaf). Russo-Baltique commercial vehicles, models D, M and T.

THE RUSSO-BALT D24/35, 1912.
ENGINE SIMILAR TO THAT
OF THE M24/35.
FOUR SPEEDS.
CARDAN DRIVE.
CARRYING CAPACITY—1 t.
WHEELBASE—3,375 mm.
TOP SPEED—40 kph.
KERB WEIGHT—1,600 kg.

THE RUSSO-BALT T40/65, 1912.
FOUR CYLINDERS—7,850 cc.
ENGINE POWER—65 hp.
FOUR SPEEDS.
CHAIN TRANSMISSION.
CARRYING CAPACITY—5—6 t.
WHEELBASE—3,650 mm.
TOP SPEED—20 kph.
KERB WEIGHT—4,220 kg.

THE RUSSO-BALT M24/35, 1911.
FOUR CYLINDERS—4,501 cc.
ENGINE POWER—35 hp.
FOUR SPEEDS.
CHAIN TRANSMISSION.
CARRYING CAPACITY—2 t.
WHEELBASE—3,400 mm.
TOP SPEED—20 kph.
KERB WEIGHT—1,920 kg.

OTHER MANUFACTURING ENTERPRISES OPERATING IN RUSSIA

Apart from the Russo-Baltic Waggon Works in Riga, a facility that was arguably the major maker of transport related products in Imperial Russia – building aeroplanes, railway rolling stock, cars and trucks, as well as general engineering items – there were a number of other concerns involved in the output of motorcycles, passenger cars, trucks, tractors and aero-engines in the decade prior to the onset of war in 1914. Some production did manage to carry on after that date and up to the Revolution in 1917; thereafter stagnation set in, and it was not until the Bolshevik regime settled down following the end of the so-called 'War of Intervention' in 1922 that thoughts turned to the reincarnation of the motor industry in the newly formed Union of Soviet Socialist Republics (USSR). Unfortunately all of the progress achieved in the private sector in Imperial times was, mainly, nullified, and therefore there came a need to start from scratch. The start at the AMO Works in Moscow in 1924 was consolidated by the inception of the first five-year plan in 1927 by Josef Stalin with the help of Henry Ford and other, mostly American, industrialists. This part of Chapter 2 examines the various manufacturers, large and small, that made up the industry from 1896 to c. 1915.

I. THE AKSAI FARM MACHINERY WORKS, ROSTOV-ON-DON

This company, as its title implies, was concerned with the production of farm implements, agricultural tools and the like, but in 1903 it considered entering into the motorcar market. They opted for licence building of established designs from overseas and they looked around for a suitable vehicle that would be satisfactory for use on the poor Russian roads of the time. The firm chose the well-known Curved-Dash Oldsmobile as its prototype, and tooled up for full-scale production accordingly. This Oldsmobile model was ideally suited for Russian conditions as it was of simple construction, rugged and well built, and possessed a high ground clearance; it was also a reliable and proven machine which had enjoyed a good sales record in the USA. The prospects looked good and Aksai advertised two models, of 6 and 8hp, building all of the components, except tyres and electrical equipment, in-house.

As is well known, the Curved-Dash Oldsmobile, invented by Ransom E. Olds of Lansing, Michigan, was a sturdy single cylinder machine with its engine and the associated 2-speed epicyclic transmission, mounted amidships, horizontally, beneath the chassis frame; final drive was by chain to a differential and live axle. The weight of the Russian version was quoted at 550kg. though its American counterpart scaled only 356kg. The Aksai variant was capable of a maximum speed of 35kmh (21mph) when the engine crankshaft was revolving at 760rpm.

Great success attended the car in the USA – 16,000 units were sold between 1901 and 1904 at a price of $650 each. Unfortunately that success did not rub off on the Aksai firm for it completed only 20 cars in 1903 before turning over to the

manufacture of aero-engines later on. These aero-engines were probably either Gnome 'Monosoupape' or Le Rhône models under licence as most of the aviation units then made in Russia were of the rotary type. It appears that they had much better success with these during the run-up to World War I. Eventually, the Aksai Farm Machinery Works was absorbed into the large Soviet conglomeration known as Rostelmash, which now produces combine harvesters under the Kolos nameplate.

References to the Curved-Dash Oldsmobile in other literature

The Autocar – 1st September 1902.
The Automotor Journal – 8th, 15th and 22nd August 1903.
Motor Vehicles & Motors – V. Worby Beaumont, vol. II, Constable London – 1906.
The Oldtime Automobile – John Bentley, Fawcett Publications, Book no. 134, Greenwich, Connecticut, USA – 1952.
The Treasury of Early American Automobiles – Floyd Clymer, Bonanza Books, div. Crown Publishers Inc, New York – 1950 (also published by McGraw-Hill).

II. BROMLEY MACHINE TOOL WORKS, MOSCOW

The proprietor of this enterprise, N. E. Bromley, is known to have considered entering the passenger car market, but no firm evidence has emerged as to type, production run or other details.

III. THE DUX BICYCLE WORKS, KHODYNKA, MOSCOW

In 1896 some foreign firms exhibited and demonstrated a number of motor bicycles and tricycles at the Khodynka Cycle Track in Moscow, where these machines were offered for sale to the Russian general public. By 1900 Yuri Alexandrovich Meller (sometimes spelt in the German manner Möller) had set up a factory on the Khodynka site to build bicycles, and this facility was expanded to cater for the production of cars, hotel buses, motorcycles, and finally, aircraft.

In the very early 1900s the organisation had been contacted by an engineer named Alexandr Basilevsky to assist him with the construction of a steam-driven, three-wheeled horseless carriage; the actual date for the completion of this vehicle is not clear, but some authorities indicate that it was ready by 1903. There is a possibility that Basilevsky was associated with the Dux Factory in some way, and as the plant had taken up a licence to build the Curved-Dash Oldsmobile, and as Ransom E. Olds had also made a three-wheeled steamer himself, the Russian may have been influenced in that direction somehow; however, this is but conjecture on the part of the writer.

Whilst the history of Basilevsky's Steam Car is unclear, there is evidence that the Dux works did produce a batch of electrically propelled 'hotel buses' in 1902. These buses were similar in form to the traditional horse-drawn hotel bus, but were strengthened to take the strain of mechanical propulsion; an example of one of these Dux buses is depicted in Fig. 23, where such a carriage

Rossiya of 1901.
4.5 hp engine.
500 cc displacement volume.
Weight 400 kg. 4 seats.
Maximum speed 35 kph.

Freze of 1902.
8 hp engine.
864 cc
displacement volume.
Weight,
about 600 kg.
4 seats.
Maximum speed
60 kph.

Aksai and Dux
produced types
under licence
from Oldsmobile
between 1903
and 1906.

The cycle-car
built by Ivan Yushkov
in 1915 with
a 6-hp motorcycle
two-cylinder engine.

Plate 9. Light cars made in Czarist times – Aksai, Dux, Freze Rossiya and Ivan Yushkov's cycle car.

is shown in the service of the Bristol Hotel. From the illustration it can be seen that the vehicle has wooden artillery wheels (shod with pneumatic tyres), Ackermann steering, full-elliptical leaf springing, and final drive by pitch-chains directly from a sprocket attached to the motor armature shaft. The motor was installed under the fore part of the bodywork in an enclosed casing that extended to the extreme rear, presumably to accommodate the battery bank. Brake drums were fitted to each rear wheel, and these were actuated by means of a hand lever; the other controls were just a steering wheel and a pedal control to the rheostat. Some approximate dimensions have been published for these buses as follows: length overall – 4300mm; width – 1900mm; height – 2700mm. The wheelbase was 2850mm. The Dux hotel bus could accommodate ten passengers, with their luggage carried on the roof in a railed grid; it was capable of a maximum speed of 20kmh or about 12mph, and it had a range of 60km when fully charged.

In 1904 Meller decided to make passenger cars, and like Aksai he also opted for licence production; again, he chose the Curved-Dash Oldsmobile for precisely the same reasons as the firm in Rostov-on-Don had. Meller named his version of the American car the Duxmobile, and he had considerably more success than Aksai did, selling 200 between 1904 and 1906. The car, as designed by Ransom E. Olds, rose to fame on the international scene, and there was even a song written about it entitled *My Merry Oldsmobile*; it was licence-built in Europe in at least three countries: Russia, as has been noted; Germany, as the Polymobil by the Polyphon Musik-Werke AG in Wahren (a noted maker of the Polyphon mechanical music box using slotted disks), and as the Ultramobil by the Deutsche Ultramobile GmbH factory in Berlin-Halensee; and, lastly, by the Swiss concern Motorwagenfabrik Excelsior in Wollishofen. The Excelsior was, however, modified by the firm's engineer, Rudolf Egg.

Having dabbled with steam, and having had some success with electricity and internal combustion engined cars, Meller then decided to enter the motorcycle market and, once again, he chose to build another manufacturer's wares under licence. The prototype that was chosen was a very basic affair, the Swiss designed Moto-Reve 275 of 1906. The Dux version was a single-speed, belt driven model that was more or less identical to its Geneva parent (Fig. A, Plate 10, p49). The cycle parts consisted of an unsprung frame that was made entirely in the Russian factory, as were the wheels, the mudguarding and the brass fuel tank. Certain components were of foreign origin, being bought out probably from Germany, and these were generally proprietary items such as pedals and lighting sets, which were of the acetylene gas pattern. The Dux motorcycle had direct belt-drive with a jockey-wheel tensioner and cycle-type braking on the rear wheel only, and was fitted with a standard cycle tubular frame. The engine, which was supplied from Switzerland, was air-cooled and operated on the four-stroke principle with automatic

inlet valves and mechanically operated side exhaust valves; the bore and stroke measurements were 50 x 70mm, which gave the engine a swept volume of 274.8cc. Later on, probably in 1912, the capacity was increased to 294cc and this increased the power output from 2bhp to 2.5bhp; when this modification occurred it is possible that Dux itself was making the power unit.

The Dux-Motoreve was capable of a maximum speed of 50kmh (about 30mph); it was produced in Moscow from 1908 until the outbreak of World War I and about 100 of them were believed to have been made annually. The construction of the Dux motorcycle closely followed that of the only other Czarist offering, the Rossiya from A. Leitner's Riga factory, and both were of a primitive nature with little or no protection from the weather or provision for comfort whatsoever; even by 1914 both types still exhibited the basic features of European motorcycles that had been offered to the public a decade earlier! In fact, they just fulfilled the role of personal transport within the limits of urban areas.

The Dux Vee-twin cylinder motorcycle – c. 1909 to c. 1914	
Manufacturer:	Yuri Alexandrovich Meller (Möller) Aktsionernoe Obshchestvo (Ltd. Co.) Dux.
Branch office:	Office & Factory – Tverskaya Zastava & Yamskaya Slobodka, Moscow. Showrooms at Neglinnai Ploshad (Square) St. Petersburg – Nevskaya no. 1559 & Moiki St.
Mechanical details:	Air-cooled Moto-Reve Vee-Twin Engine 50mm bore x 70mm stroke, four-cycle with automatic inlet valves and side exhaust. 274.8cc (later increased to 294cc), 2bhp in original form, increased to 2.5 magneto ignition.
Frame:	Strengthened, tubular cycle type.
Transmission:	Direct belt drive to rear wheel using jockey tensioner. Free engine position using exhaust-valve lifter.
Wheels:	Bicycle type with pneumatic tyres.
Brakes:	Cable operated rim brakes to rear wheel only.
Equipment:	Sprung leather saddle, fuel tank under crossbar, leather tool bag etc., mudguards standard fitting but acetylene lighting an optional extra.
Weight:	2 poods (32.76kg or about 72lb).
Performance:	Speed variation – 6 to 60 versts per hour. 6.04 to 60.4kmh (about 3½ to 37mph).
Price:	Ryb.380 as described above.
Other data:	About 100 of these machines were produced annually at the Dux Moscow plant and probably 400 units were actually supplied.

Fig. 23. The Dux electrically-propelled hotel bus.

Also, in the period just before World War I, the Dux organisation produced a motorised sledge propelled by an airscrew, which was driven by a small petrol engine mounted at the rear. Apart from the picture (Fig. 25), which is taken from an advertisement, the writer is unaware of any other details concerning it.

The overall history of the Velozavod Dux, as it was known in Russian, is interesting. From its inception as a mere cycle factory, it eventually became one of the major suppliers of aviation equipment and aircraft in Imperial Russia, and a prominent component of the Soviet aircraft industry.

Following the exhibition of the foreign motorcycles at the Khodynka Cycle Track in 1896, where all of the machines on show were priced at Ryb.500 or more (£200), Meller considered he could make a domestic item at a more realistic

sum. Consequently he erected a workshop nearby the track, initially to build ordinary pedal cycles, but eventually to break into the automobile and motorcycle business. This goal was achieved with relative success during the first decade of the 20th century, despite the problems that always seemed to beset industry in Czarist times. Probably Yuri Meller realised that motor engineering in Russia would not make his fortune, but he, obviously, aimed for higher things; it was in 1910 or 1911 that he equipped his plant to build aircraft, and from that time onwards he reduced motorcycle output gradually.

With the enterprise turned over to aircraft production, a Chief Engineer and Designer named F. E. Moska was employed in those capacities. The primary course of action was to create an indigenous industry and this route was, indeed, partially successful. Nevertheless, other forces did cause a return to

Fig. 24. Reproduction from a page of the Dux catalogue, showing a view of the Motoreve-Dux Machine that was built by Yuri Alexandrovich Meller in Moscow from circa 1910 to 1913.

Fig. 24a. Surviving Dux model fitted with Vee-twin Motoreve 2hp engine. It is believed to date from 1912 and is seen in this picture at the Riga Motorcycle '85 Rally. (Courtesy J. Ramba)

licence building when the war began in 1914. The first aeroplane to be made in the Dux works was the Dux-Farman, which was a modified French, Maurice Farman design; however, by 1913, four domestic machines had been constructed to Moska's specifications. These were as follows:

The Dux-II: A pusher-engined monoplane which was possibly the first Russian-designed aeroplane to be built in a Russian factory.

The Möller-I – Similar to the Dux-II, but made specifically to carry a machine gun. (NB: All three of the Möller machines were designated in the German manner in written texts.)

The Möller-II – A pusher biplane intended for military use, and which was involved in a bizarre accident. The incident occurred at the 1913 War Ministry Trials when the Möller-II was flying in company with the Sikorsky Russki-Vityaz, one of the four-engined giants from the Russo-Baltic Works. The rotary engine fitted to the Möller-II tore itself free from its mountings, hurtling down and hitting the larger aeroplane, which promptly crashed, killing all on board. The Möller pilot escaped to land the engineless plane as a glider!

Fig. 25. The Motor-Sledge manufactured by the Dux Bicycle Works. The Russian text indicates that the machine is a cross between an aeroplane and a metal chassis, drawn through the air by draught from the propeller.

The Möller-III – this was the final Moska designed machine, a monoplane with twin propellers driven by shafts from a centrally mounted 80hp Salmson radial engine. It was the last Dux designed aeroplane to be manufactured. It did not work too well, but a similar machine, the Salmson-Moineau SM1, was better, and was sent to Russia in 1917.

Yuri Meller did not normally build engines to power his aircraft, tending to use Gnome rotary units which were assembled in Russia at the Gnome-Rhone Engine Works in a factory established in 1912 at a site in the Moscow area, probably at Fili where a number of expatriate firms were at work. This plant imported components from France, and it assembled engines in large numbers in order to supply the needs of most of the aircraft manufacturers in Imperial Russia. After the Bolshevik Revolution the facility became known as the State Factory No. 2.

Meller did build one engine, however, and this was of an experimental nature, being made to designs and specifications supplied by A. V. Nesterov in 1914; this engine was a radial, water-cooled unit having 7 cylinders, each with a bore and stroke of 140 x 164.3mm to give a swept volume of 17.3 litres. Its power output was 120hp, it weighed 164kg, its overall diameter was 1260mm and its length, from the airscrew boss to the mounting plate, was 1250mm. It was given the name Hipotsikl Nesterov and it still exists today in the collection of the Air-Force Museum at Monino (Fig. 28a).

In 1914, with the need to produce aeroplanes in some quantity to service the needs of the armed forces in wartime, Yuri

Plate 10. Dux motorcycles.

"ДУКСЪ"

MAK.

ВЕЛО
ЗАВОД
ДУКСЪ

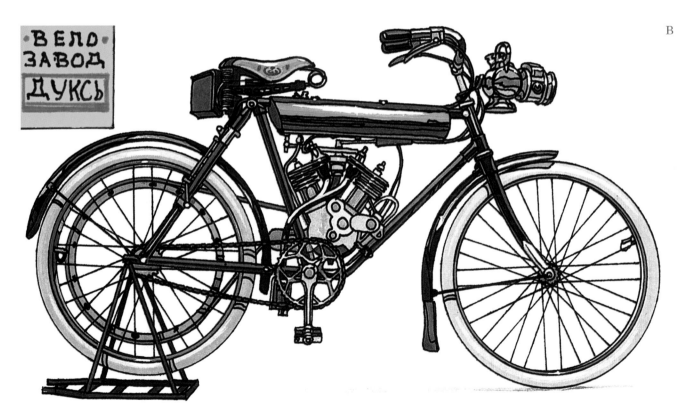

Meller, once more, returned to building under licence; he chose known and reliable prototypes, all of French origin, and during the years throughout World War I up to the outbreak of the Revolution in 1917, these aircraft, notably from Bleriot, Farman, Nieuport, and later on Morane, were supplied continuously. Unfortunately when the Provisional Government under Kerensky took power in March of 1917, apathy set in and most industrial production came to a complete halt; nevertheless, in November of 1918, the Bolsheviks established the Peoples' Commissariat for the Collegium of the Air-Force (NKKAF), a body which sought to restart factories that produced munitions, motor vehicles, aircraft and railway equipment as well as repair workshops. How production fared during the years of the War of Intervention (the civil war that involved troops sent from governments all over Europe) has not been recorded properly, and the next that is known of the Dux Works is that it had been re-commissioned as a centre for research and development into aviation by the Soviet government in 1920 or thereabouts. One of the first programmes that the Dux factory undertook occurred in 1922 for a leading aeronautical expert of the times, Professor N. Zhukovskii, who had headed up a team as the newly formed Commission for Heavy Aviation (Kommissi po Tyazheloi Aviatskii – Komta) in 1919 to develop a new heavy transport aeroplane.

This plane was named the Komta, or sometimes Kometa, and it was a large triplane transport. Although a number of them were built at the Dux plant, the machine was relatively unsuccessful. After Zhukovskii's death in 1921, the well-known aircraft designer N. Polikarpov took over both the position as head of the commission and that of Director of the Dux factory. By 1922 the plant was renamed the Osoaviakhim No. 1 Zavod, later to be contracted to just Zavod No. 1, and sometimes referred to as the First State Aircraft Factory. Osoaviakhim was a curious organisation, and its name meant "The Association of Societies for the promotion of Defense and Aero-Chemical Development"; between the wars it was responsible for many activities, ranging from the training of aviation technicians and pilots, and the creation of specialist technical training in military and civilian schools and colleges, to the promotion of flying as a sport. However, its influence was much wider than just training, for it acted as a 'patron of the art' and funded many different experimental projects, including two large semi-rigid airships which were designated the 'B5' and 'B6' and which were constructed in 1934. It also provided the backing for the first Soviet motorcycle, the Union (Soyuz), made at the former Dux works in 1924 by a team of engineers under the leadership of Peter Lvov. The influence of the Osoaviakhim permeated right throughout Soviet industry, and the association appeared to have been specifically orientated towards the needs of defence through advanced technology.

Also at the former Dux plant, Polikarpov designed the first Soviet fighter plane, the IL-400, which flew for the first time in August 1923; by 1939, Zavod No. 1 was engaged in the full production of a Polikapov fighter aircraft known as the I-153.

From the time that Yuri Meller started his bicycle factory

at the dawn of the 20th century, to his building the airfield at Khodynka in 1910, and on to the series production of aeroplanes during World War I, the Dux works had always been at the forefront of Czarist Russian industry. Whilst it is not the remit of this work to discuss aeronautics in any depth, it is important to discover how a small bicycle factory eventually became the focal point of the Soviet Space Programme; also in the time from 1910 onwards, the motor industry was closely bound up with aviation. The Dux Works and its successor, Zavod No. 1, have been witness to many of the major milestones in Russian industrial history; in 1910 B. I. Rossinsky flew the first indigenous Russian aeroplane; in 1918 V. I. Lenin observed the first Soviet Mayday Flypast, and in 1922 the first Soviet designed transport plane, the Komta, albeit un-successful, was assembled at Khodynka, whilst in 1924 the first Soviet fighter plane was made there. Also, as had been noted previously, the first motorcycle designed and built under the auspices of the leadership of the USSR was developed at Khodynka. After these beginnings the Zavod No. 1 became the cornerstone of Soviet aviation with the development and construction of specialised aircraft, sometimes in long series; the crowning moment came when Yuri Gagarin and Gherman Titov arrived at Khodynka in 1959 to inaugurate the dawn of the space age. By then the airfield and its associated laboratories had been renamed the MV Frunze Central Airport after a prominent Politburo Member, Mikhail Frunze, who was the Peoples' Commissar for Heavy Industry.

From bicycle factory to a leading space age research and development laboratory was a long journey indeed!

References to the Dux Bicycle Works in other literature

Russian Civil & Military Aircraft 1884-1969 – Heinz Nowarra & G. R. Duval Afm, Harleyford Publications, Watford – 1970. (From the Czarist historical point of view, the best review of Russian aeronautics from 1884 to 1917 in English.)

Aviatsiya V Roccii (Aviation in Russia) – M. V. Kellash, G. P. Svishchev & S. A. Khristianov, Izdatelstvo Mashinostroenie, Moscow – 1983 & 1988 (Russian text). (The most complete history of Russian Aviation from 1784-1917.)

Avtomobili Strana Sovetov (Automobiles of the Soviet Land) – L. M. Shugurov & V. P. Shirshov, Izdatelstvo Dosaaf SSSR, Moscow – 1980 (Russian text).

Avtoexport Round-up – Quarterly journal in English, formerly published by the Russian Trade Organisation V/O Avtoexport, Volkhonka, Moscow.

IV. FREZE & CO., COACHBUILDERS, ST. PETERSBURG

Peter Freze commenced operations as a coachbuilder in 1896 and he is a notable figure, inasmuch as he was one of the founding partners of the Russian Motor Industry. He collaborated with a retired naval officer, Yevgeny Yakovlev, who was the Director of the Yakovlev Kerosene & Gas Engine Works in St. Petersburg. This firm concentrated on the manufacture of stationary oil

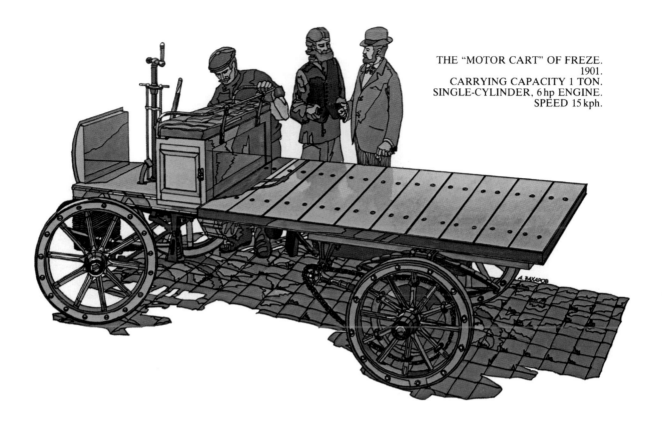

THE "MOTOR CART" OF FREZE.
1901.
CARRYING CAPACITY 1 TON.
SINGLE-CYLINDER, 6 hp ENGINE.
SPEED 15 kph.

Fig. 26. The 1-ton truck made by Peter Freze (seen in the right of the picture, in the trilby hat) in 1902. The engine and gearbox came from De Dion Bouton but the rest was made in the Freze factory in St. Petersburg. Twenty examples were actually manufactured.

and gas engines as prime movers for industry. Yakovlev's knowledge of internal combustion engines, together with the coach-building expertise of Freze, made the partnership ideal for the production of a motorcar during the last decade of the 19th century. The vehicle is illustrated in Fig. 8 and in Plate 1.

As may be seen from the illustrations, the vehicle was of the 'dog-cart' variety, and was designed, presumably, along Benz lines like the old Nesseldorf from Bohemia and the Lutzmann and the Orient Express from Germany. Licence-built Benz 'dog-carts' were also produced in England as the Arnold-Benz, in France as the Roger-Benz, and in the USA as the Mueller-Benz.

The partnership of Yakovlev and Freze was, indeed, symbiotic, for without one the other could not have manufactured the car. The engine and transmission were made at the Yakovlev Works, whilst the frame, springs, wheels and carriage-work were constructed by Peter Freze.

The overall construction of the vehicle was, more or less, identical to that of the 1894 Benz single-cylinder machine. The Russian car had a capacity of 860cc and its 'one-lung' produced between 1.5 and 2bhp; the design of this engine was more in line with stationary engine practice rather than that of an automotive unit; transmission was initially by use of a flat belt but, unlike the Benz, the Russian vehicle only had one road speed. The belt drove a countershaft, possibly by means of a 'fast and loose' double pulley system, and sprockets attached to the extremities of this shaft were connected to chainwheels, fixed to the spokes of the rear road wheels via final drive by pitch-chains. This was a system that had been used previously by Benz. The Yakovlev-Freze car had electric ignition, candle headlamps, and it seated two people; the wheelbase was 1370mm, the weight about 300kg, and it was capable of a maximum speed of 20kmh (roughly 13mph).

This early motorcar was exhibited at the All-Russia Industrial Art Exhibition in 1896 at Nizhny-Novgorod, where it attracted a great deal of attention, being the first such vehicle to be shown to the general public in Russia.

After building the 'dog-cart' in 1896, Peter Freze must have specialised in the provision of coachwork on other manufacturers' chassis for a few years, as the next vehicle from this maker did not appear until 1902, some six years later. Two vehicles were advertised for 1902, a rather elegant rear-door tonneau akin to the then current De Dion Bouton

Fig. 27. An open charabanc body fitted to the 1-ton Freze chassis. Built in 1903.

cars, and a flat platform, 1-ton truck. The passenger car was reputedly modelled on the 8hp De Dion tourer of the day, but its bodywork was of better proportions than its French counterpart. As far as the writer knows there was no licence agreement between Freze and the French firm, but the Russian enterprise always used De Dion Bouton engines and gearboxes from 1902 onwards. This car is illustrated in Plate 8. The truck, shown in Fig. 26, was a very spartan affair with no consideration whatsoever for driver comfort. It could carry a payload of 1 ton and its 6hp De Dion engine was placed beneath the drivers seat. The three-speed gearbox drove a countershaft and the sprockets attached to this shaft carried the drive to the rear wheels by side chains. This truck had a maximum speed of 16kmh, or just over 10mph, and 20 units were actually manufactured. Four of these commercial vehicles were demonstrated in the Military Manoeuvres At Kursk in 1902, whilst a charabanc style bus was built on a chassis in 1903 (Fig. 27). A fire appliance was also built in 1904. Both of these Freze motor vehicles were current from 1902 to 1904, after which it seems that the firm returned to its mainstream business of coach-building. Some dimensions etc., are noted here:

1902 4-seat, rear tonneau Freze passenger car	
Engine:	8hp single cylinder De Dion Bouton. (8bhp at 2000rpm). Capacity 864cc.
Gearbox:	2-speed, final drive by shaft.
Weight:	600kg.
1902 1-ton flat platform truck	
Engine:	6 or 8hp De Dion Bouton as for passenger car (6hp power unit gave 6bhp / 4.5kw at 2000rpm).
Gearbox:	3-speed, final drive by side chains.
Dimensions:	Wheelbase – 2220mm. Length overall – 3200mm. Height overall – 1620mm. Wheel diameter – 720mm.
Wheel type:	Wooden artillery with iron tyres.
Controls:	Tiller steering, gear-change and throttle beneath tiller, hand-brake and reverse drive crank to right of driver.

V. T. KALEP, THE MOTOR WORKS, AVIATION DEPARTMENT, RIGA & MOSCOW

The Motor Works in Riga concentrated on the production of engines for aeronautical purposes, and the proprietor is credited with the introduction of the first Russian designed and built aero-engine in 1911. However, another pioneer, A. G. Ufimtsev, whose name is sometimes linked with that of Kalep, did obtain Russian patents for a radial form of engine in 1908 and 1911. These were patent no. 1997 of 9th February 1908, and patent no. 38313 of 13th October 1911.

Ufimtsev originally made a twin-cylinder, two-stroke engine that weighed 40kg and produced between 15 and 20hp. Later on he built his own aeroplane of a curious configuration, which was named the Spheroplane and had an annular wing formation; this was thought to have been fitted with the 20hp engine, and

is known to have been unsuccessful. Following on from the 1910 effort, Spheroplane-2 was built in 1911 and this, also, did not fly. Ufimtsev then produced the six-cylinder engine shown in Fig. 28b which was built for him at the Briansk Locomotive Works. This power unit had a cylinder bore of 100mm and a stroke of 120mm. It weighed 58kg and had a capacity of 5.6 litres, producing between 65 and 75bhp at 1000rpm. The engine was exhibited at the 2nd International Air Exhibition between 25th March and 8th April 1912 in Moscow. This engine exists in the collection of the Air Force Museum at Monino. Whether or not Ufimtsev influenced Kalep is open to conjecture but the latter also had aero-engine patents attributed to him and these are nos. 25056 and 25057 of 30th September 1913, designated Class 46d.

The aero-engines made by T. Kalep were in a K-series and were as follows:

The K-35 – possibly the original unit of 1910, 35bhp at 1500rpm.

The K-60 – 110mm bore x 120mm stroke, 60bhp at 1200rpm. Weight 66kg.

The K-80 – 124mm bore x 140mm stroke, 80bhp at 1200rpm. 7 cylinders. Weight 110kg.

The K-100 – 124mm bore x 150mm stroke, 100bhp at 1200rpm. 7 cylinders. Weight: 110kg.

Production figures for these engines as given in Russian sources are not conclusive but it appears that the K-60 type had a run of 100 units from 1913 to 1st August 1915; in a similar period only 38 examples of the K-80 were made, and up to 1917 only 330 units were manufactured in total. However, the output of the factory including the license-built engines seemed to have been from 500 to 1000 engines per annum, during the war years.

The writer has only managed to pinpoint two actual examples which were fitted to specific aircraft. One of them, the Delphin (Dolphin) was designed by V. V. Dybovski in 1913 and this aircraft was a very streamlined monoplane that was well ahead of its time. It was fitted with a K-80 power unit. The other example was the Sikorski S-16 Scout, serial no. 156, which had a K-60 engine installed.

An example of the Kalep K-80 engine remains in the collection of the Air Force Museum at Monino.

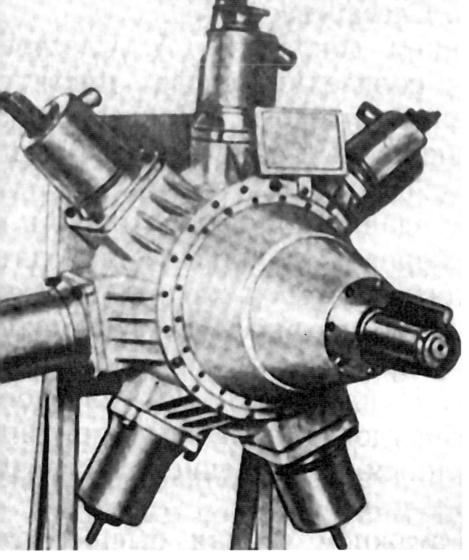

Fig. 28a. Aero-engines made in Imperial Russia: 7-cylinder, liquid cooled, radial engine made by A. V. Nesterov. (A. B. Hecтepoв)

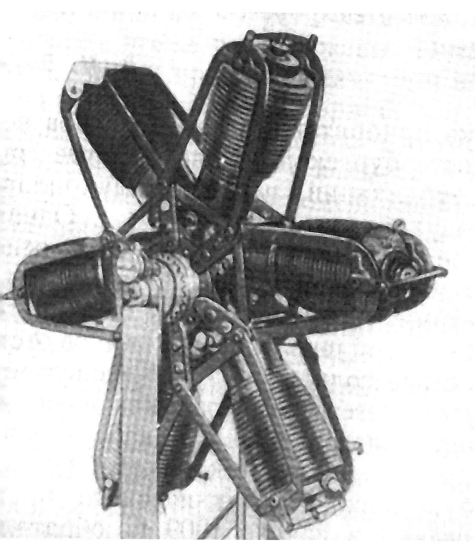

Fig. 28b. Aero-engines made
in Imperial Russia: 6-cylinder,
air-cooled, rotary engine made by
A. G. Ufimtsev. (А УФИМЦЕВ)

The Yaroslavl location is known to have produced about 200 trucks that were based upon a Fiat design, probably that of the 7.4-litre, 5-ton model. Another vehicle that was styled as the 'Lebed-A' was of English origin, being a licensed copy of the legendary Crossley RFC-Tender, which had been introduced in its native land for airfield liaison use in 1912.

However, V. A. Lebedev was not really interested in the manufacture of road vehicles, having had a great penchant for aviation. He founded St. Petersburg Aviation Ltd. in 1915 or 1916 to assist in the war effort, having previously made a number of aircraft to foreign specifications elsewhere. These earlier machines were mainly derivatives of the Albatros Werke GmbH but by 1915, supplies of parts etc. from Germany had dried up and other avenues had to be explored. Over the next couple of years, at the three plants at Taranrog, Penza and in the capital, a whole range of aeroplanes was built ranging from the Lebed-I to the final type, the Lebed-XXIV in 1917. These factories, together with the Yaroslavl plant, seem to have survived the war and the Revolution intact, for it has been noted that further types including the experimental float-plane, the Lebed-LM1 (based upon the Lebed-XI) were made on into Soviet times. The Yaroslavl installation became a motor repair depot during the earlier part of the 1920s, being re-named as the Yaroslavl Avto-Remontnogo Zavod, (Yaroslavl Auto-Repair Factory), later on to become one of the foremost truck plants in the Soviet Union, the Yaroslavl Avtomobil Zavod, (Yaroslavl Automobile Factory.)

Whilst a number of Russian firms made aero-engines between 1913 and the onset of the Revolution in 1917, it appears that only the Motor Works concentrated its efforts on this form of prime mover.

VI. VLADIMIR ALEXANDROVICH LEBEDEV, ZAVOD LEBED, YAROSLAVL, ST. PETERSBURG (PETROGRAD), TARANROG & PENZA. ST. PETERSBURG AVIATSKAYA ORGANICHENIE (ST. PETERSBURG AVIATION LTD.)

The main plant operated by V. A. Lebedev was a reasonably sized facility at Yaroslavl; nevertheless, its importance on the motor vehicle scene in Czarist Russia was limited, for its prime source of output was the manufacture of foreign vehicles under licence, a policy that was prevalent in that era. The three other factories were all concerned with the production of aircraft.

VII. ALEXANDR LEITNER, THE ROSSIYA VELOSOPEDNOI FABRIK, (THE RUSSIAN BICYCLE WORKS), RIGA

Leitner, unlike Lebedev, was an important figure in the Czarist motor vehicle arena, for he was a talented engineer and one of the real pioneers of the industry before World War I. He commenced his career in a similar way to that of Yuri Meller, by building pedal cycles. He was born in 1864 in Kurland, which is now in present day Latvia, and he was of German descent;

Fig. 29. De Dion type tricycle, as made by A. Leitner of Riga. Five were built along these lines in 1899.

his surname was originally spelt in the Teutonic fashion, Leutner. Initially, Leitner strove to improve his knowledge of cycle construction by touring Europe to see how the industry operated in other countries; he went to Coventry, at that time the centre of the cycle industry in the UK, and then went on to France and Germany. Eventually, he set himself up in business in Gertrude Street, Riga in 1886, and in the first year at that address he managed to employ four staff to make a total of 19 'ordinary' or penny-farthing bicycles.

Things obviously went well, for in 1890, having outgrown the Gertrude Street premises, he moved to a larger facility in Suvorov Street which had three-storey accommodation; now

he was employing 60 workmen, and producing 500 bicycles each year under the Rossiya nameplate.

It appears that Leitner did not wish to remain just a bicycle manufacturer, and needed to move on to much higher levels. His interest in motorcycles began in 1895 at the same time that, once again, he moved factory. This time he went to Nos. 129 and 131 Alexander Street, Riga, his last before the outbreak of World War I; later on he acquired Nos. 132 and 133 as well. Also in this year, 1895, Leitner tried out a German motorcycle, the Hildebrand & Wolfmüller, which was made in Munich to Deutsches Reich, patent no. 78553 of 1892; originally, this German pioneer motorcycle was quite popular in Europe and over its three years of production, some 2000 units were made and sold. Unfortunately the Hildebrand had a number of problems that were never ironed out and the initial enthusiasm for the model soon waned. However, in Russia alone there were three dealerships for this machine, and its popularity even permeated as far east as Odessa where one example remains to this day. Leitner was not at all impressed by the Hildebrand, and therefore looked around for a more suitable type of motorcycle for series output.

In 1898 Leitner went to St. Petersburg to witness some motorcycle trials that were held in the capital, and which were even styled as a race. Here he became enthusiastic about the performance of some De Dion engined tricycles of the Clement type that were being demonstrated. Consequently, in 1899 he obtained some 1.75hp De Dion engines and applied them to his standard tricycle frames, which were suitably strengthened to take them. In the event he made five of these three-wheelers, and one of them is depicted in Fig. 29.

Leitner was still without a product to manufacture and sell, and he approached Eugene and Michel Werner in Paris in order to conclude a licence agreement for their new style motorcycle which had just come out for the 1901 season. The Werner Frères were emigré Russian journalists who had decided that motorcycle design and construction would be more lucrative, and accordingly set up in business in the Avenue de Grand Armée in Paris during 1897; originally they had positioned the power unit over the front wheel of the cycle, but this had made the machine un-stable and difficult to handle as well as being positively dangerous due to having hot-tube ignition. The 'New Werner Position' where the engine was set in the frame between the wheels became an instant success, and had not both of the brothers died by 1904, the company would probably not have faded out by 1908. Leitner soon realised the potential of the 'new' Werner and he started to produce the two-wheeler in 1902. The Russian machines were fitted with the 2hp Fafnir engine which has supplanted the Labitte unit used by the Werners, and this German product was made by the Aachner Stahlware Fabrik AG later to become Fafnirwerke AG.

Notwithstanding his entry into the powered vehicle market, Leitner continued to make pedal cycles which were of excellent quality, so much so, that he received a Diploma of Honour at the 1901 International Exhibition in Glasgow.

At more or less the same time as Leitner had made the arrangements to produce the licence-built Werner motorcycle, he had also made contact with Max Cudell of Aachen in order to build his De Dion based cars under license. In fact, these cars were identical to the 1899 3.5hp Voiturette De Dion Bouton, and they were made under a licence granted by the French firm to Cudell. Nevertheless, Leitner managed to obtain rights to the manufacture of the car and produced them at a rate of 10 units per annum. (If Leitner built them up to 1908, then 60 vehicles may be a probable total.) One of these Rossiya motorcars was exhibited at the Riga Jubilee Exhibition of 1901 where it won a top award; this was certain

to have been the prototype from the Riga factory. At first the standard 3.5 De Dion motor was utilised, but later Fafnir engines were fitted.

Between 1908 and 1914 Leitner gained some more rights to the production of foreign vehicles, and during this period he tooled up to build the German Büssing truck models; he was also the main agent in Russia for Opel and Dixi cars as well as Michelin tyres.

In 1915 the German Army arrived at the gates of Riga and Leitner very quickly removed his factory and equipment to Kharkov where he was engaged in war work for the duration. After hostilities had ended bicycle production was resumed, though possibly Leitner had nothing to do with it, as the Soviets had taken over. By 1929 the Kharkov Cycle Works, as it had become known, was the largest enterprise of its type in the USSR, though it was still using about 90 per cent of the tooling from the Riga plant.

Another company operating in Riga, Gustav Erenpreis & Co., took over what was left of Leitner's establishment, and after World War I it became the biggest cycle producer in Latvia until the Soviets sequestered the enterprise in 1944, renaming it as the Sarkana-Zvaigzne Zavod or Red Star Works to manufacture mopeds and small motorcycles under the Riga trademark.

It is probable that Alexandr Leitner left Russia shortly after World War I, for he died and is buried in the south of Italy.

Of all of Leitner's products, only two examples remain in existence; one is an 'Ordinary' bicycle which is in a Riga Museum, whilst the other is a Rossiya Motorcycle of 1902 in private ownership. This latter vehicle is the oldest Russian self-propelled road vehicle in existence today.

Some details of the surviving Leitner Rossiya Motorcycle are as follows:

Date of manufacture:	1902
Engine details:	Fafnir, 2hp, air-cooled, single cylinder. Works no. 889. Carburettor no. 327.
Frame no:	15569
Trademarks:	Silver plated headstock badge with Rossiya logo serial no. stamped on headstock above badge. All engine components stamped with a crown plus an elegant swan marking on the crankcase and the ignition breaker cover.

Figs. 30 & 31 show details of Rossiya motorcycles, with Figs. 30 a & b depicting catalogue views of the machine, and Figs. 31 a & b showing photos of the remaining machine.

Plate 11 depicts the restored Rossiya machine of 1902.

Fig. 30b. Fafnir engine mounted in a Rossiya motorcycle. Picture taken from an old Leitner catalogue of 1903.

Fig. 30a. Rossiya type of motorcycle as made in 1903 by A. Leitner. The machine used a German Fafnir engine.

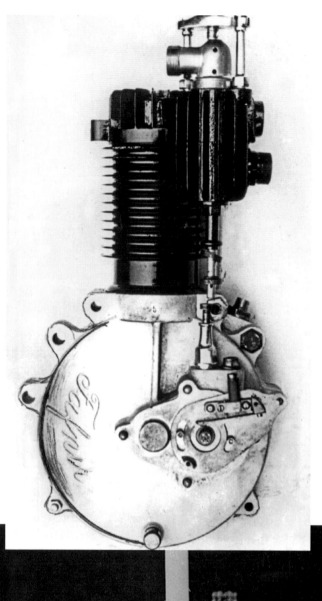

Fig. 31a. The Fafnir engine fitted to the surviving
Rossiya machine, owned by Mr. Juris Ramba, Chairman,
Motorcycle Section of the Antika Automobil Klub of
Riga. (Courtesy Seno Motociklu Sekcija AAK)

Fig. 32. The Rossiya-Cudell
motorcar that was fitted with a De
Dion Bouton engine and made by
A. Leitner in 1901.

Fig. 31b. The sole surviving Rossiya machine in
exhibition at a Riga antique vehicle rally.

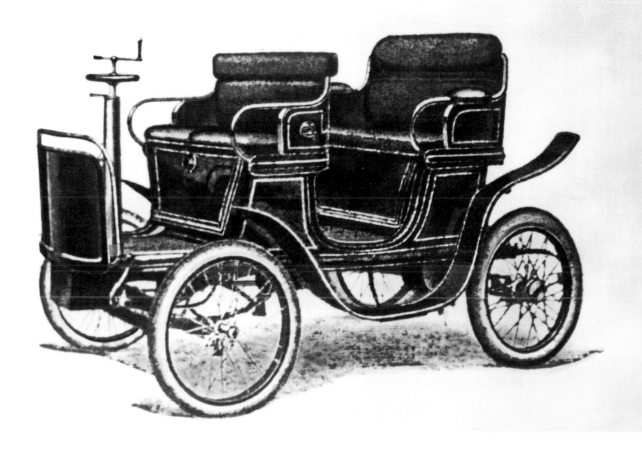

Specifications & other trade details of the Rossiya motor vehicles

The Rossiya single-cylinder motorcycle – 1902/1903	
Manufacturer:	Alexandr Leitner & Co. The Rossiya Bicycle Works. 129/131 Alexandrovskaya, Riga, Latvia, Imperial Russia.
Branch offices:	Riga – No. 7 Theatre Boulevard. St. Petersburg – No. 2 Mikhailovsk St. Moscow – Petrovskaya Avenue. Kiev – No. 3 Kreshchatik St. Warsaw – Theatre Square & No. 22 Senatovskii St. Lodz – No. 107 Petrovskaya St. Paris – 17 Rue de Paradis. The Moscow office in particular was quite palatial, whilst other offices and showrooms had extensive advertising plastered all over them.

Engine:	230cc air or water-cooled, Fafnir 4-stroke single-cylinder unit.
Bore:	65mm.
Stroke:	72mm.
Bhp:	1.75/2hp.
Ignition:	Trembler coil and breaker and dry battery.
Carburettor:	Fafnir type – single-spray with concentric float bowl.
Frame:	Specially strengthened, bicycle, tubular type.
Brakes:	Front – manual spoon type on front tyre. Rear – back-pedalling, coaster hub.
Wheels:	Wire-spoked, bicycle type with pneumatic tyres.
Equipment:	Sprung leather saddle, battery & coil slung between crossbar frames, surface carburettor, fuel & oil tanks behind seat tube (note that tank is situated under crossbar in restored example). Mudguards a standard fitment.

The Rossiya single-cylinder motorcycle – 1902/1903 (cont.)

Transmission: Weight: Performance:	Single speed, belt drive. 100lb. 6 to 40 versts per hour.
Translation of 1902 advertisement:	This motor bicycle has been built using our long experience in the field of the art of motoring and motorcycling. The workmanship of the machine is to the most accurate standard and its equipment is of the latest type with the appropriate accessories. In view of Russia's poor roads we have ensured that the frame is of extra strength, made using the best seamless tubes; it encloses the engine in a loop beneath the crankcase. Petrol engine of 1¾hp – of the best construction and workmanship with an aluminium crankcase. Ignition by electric battery. Automatic belt tensioning. Free wheel with back-pedal brake. Front wheel by stirrup brake. Low overall ratio for easy pedalling if engine has failed. Speed 6 to 40 versts per hour. Water-cooled engine optional.
Price:	Standard model with roundbelt and pneumatic tyres: Ryb.425. De-luxe model with flat belt and wider tyres: Ryb.450. De-luxe model with flat belt and wider tyres & water-cooled engine: Ryb.475.

Awards for Rossiya bicycles

Gold medals	Nizhni-Novgorod 1896. St. Petersburg 1899.
Silver medals	Kursk 1895. Pskov 1895.

The Rossiya-Cudell motorcar

Title of company:	Russia-Fahrradwerke und Automobilfabrik, A Leutner & Co., "The Oldest and Greatest Bicycle Works in Russia." The address given was no. 129/131 Alexanderstrasse Riga.
Engine: Bore: Stroke: Bhp:	De Dion Type, single-cylinder with automatic inlet valve and air-cooling. 90mm. 110mm. 4.5 @ 2000rpm.
Frame:	Tubular, bicycle type.
Gearbox:	Two-speed with optional reverse.
Final drive:	Shaft with De Dion type axle.

Plate 11. The Rossiya motorcycle preserved by Mr. Juris Ramba. (Courtesy J. Ramba)

A German advertisement for the Rossiya car dated 1901 stated the following information:

"Grand Prix Award at the Rigaer Jubiläums-Austellung 1901.
No. of velocipedes manufactured (i.e. Ordinary) – 350
No. of bicycles manufactured – 5000"

References to Rossiya vehicles in other literature

Auto Mobila Vestures Lappuses – E. Liepins, Zinatne, Riga – 1983.
Russian Motorbicycles from Riga, Alexander Leutner's Cycle Manufactory, its History and Products – Juris Ramba, Chairman Antique Automobil Klub, Riga – 1984.
Avtoexport Round-up – Quarterly journal of the former trade organisation of the USSR V/O Avtoexport, Volhonka, Moscow.

The writer is indebted to Juris Ramba for providing all of the illustrations and text for this entry.

VIII. G. A. LESSNER ENGINEERING, BOILER & IRON WORKS, ST. PETERSBURG

This firm, founded by Grigory Lessner in the 19th century, was a fairly large enterprise located in the capital, concentrating on the manufacture of machine tools, boilers and steam engines as its title indicates. However, in the first decade of the 20th century Lessner decided to enter the vehicle market, and to effect this move he chose a young Russian, Boris Lutsky, to be a consultant and designer for his company. Lutsky was well versed in car design as he had spent a number of years in Germany working mainly for Daimler-Marienfelde, where he had been involved in the design side of the truck arm of the Daimler Motoren Gesellschaft in Canstatt-Marienfelde, Berlin. (Cars from this firm were known as Mercedes from 1901 onwards but the commercial vehicles retained the old title until 1914.)

Boris Lutsky was instrumental in the introduction of mechanical transport into Russia when, in 1901, he brought two 5-ton Daimler-Marienfelde trucks to carry goods from the Izhorsky Zavod in the district of Kolpino to St. Petersburg; these trucks and their performance evoked a great deal of interest amongst industrialists in Czarist Russia, and as a result of their prowess Lessner signed an agreement with the German firm to manufacture Daimler products and to hire Lutsky as his designer.

By 1904 Grigory Lessner had built his first Daimler licensed unit, a fire-fighting appliance, whose chassis was identical to the 1901 Marienfelde design and to the Milnes-Daimlers that were sold in Great Britain by G. F. Milnes & Co. Ltd. of Wellington, Shropshire, being fitted with his bodies (mainly omnibuses).

The following year, 1905, the Lessner firm received its first series order, from the St. Petersburg post office; this request was for a batch of 14 Mail Vans shown in Fig. 36. These vans were made along passenger car lines and were fitted with 8hp twin-cylinder water-cooled engines, sliding pinion gearboxes and final drive by sprockets and chains; the vehicles were capable of a maximum speed of 30kmh or about 18mph. These

THE LESSNER PASSENGER
CAR WITH FOUR-CYLINDER
22 hp ENGINE (1907).

THE LESSNER VAN
WITH A PAYLOAD
OF 1200KG (1908).

Fig. 33. A Daimler-Marienfelde truck that was supplied to an English firm, but which was similar to the 5-ton version made by Boris Lutskoi in 1904.

vans remained in service with the postal authorities for a number of years and they were reported to have been reliable performers. At the 1st International Automobile Exhibition held in St. Petersburg in 1907, a gearbox from one of them was exhibited to demonstrate the quality of Lessner's manufactures; this unit had two years' use and 35,000km to its credit, and it was still in excellent condition. Whilst 35,000km is not much today, it was a vast distance by the metalurgical standards of the time. Also at this exhibition, Lessner showed four vehicles – a mail van, a truck and two passenger cars, one with a 32hp power unit and one with a six-cylinder 90hp engine. The bodies for the Lessner cars were supplied by the St. Petersburg carriage builder Breitigham (see Chapter 3). For their effort at the show, Messrs Lessner were awarded the Grand Gold Medal for "the establishment of automobile production" in Russia.

Plate 12. Lessner motor vehicles.

Lessner offered a total of 13 models from 1906 to 1909, when the firm discontinued production: they were passenger cars with 12, 22, 32 and 90hp engines and 1¼ and 2-ton trucks, some of which were fitted with fire engine and omnibus bodies. The 1¼-tonners had chain drive and the 2-ton models had shaft drive.

It appears that the most popular Lessner passenger car was the Lessner-32 depicted in Fig. 37. It is shown fitted with a Roi de Belges style of open body, and the car had a distinctive period Mercedes appearance. It seems that Lessner pursued a similar course of action to that of Messrs. Smith & Mabley of 7th Avenue, New York, the manufacturer of the S & M Simplex in that whilst they used Mercedes technology, the vehicles were not exact copies of the German wares. The Lessner-32 was very similar in appearance to the Simplex-50 but the engine ratings were different to each other and to those of Daimler origin. Technical specifications of the Lessner-32 are as shown overleaf:

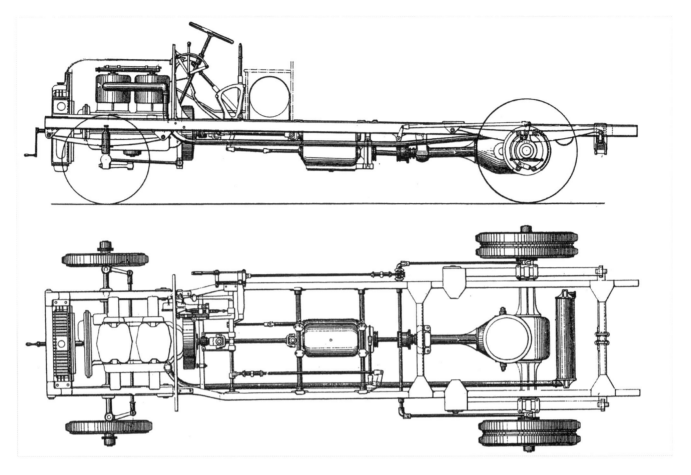

Fig. 34. Line drawings of the Daimler-Marienfelde chassis, as manufactured by G. A. Lessner Engineering Boiler & Iron Works of St. Petersburg.

Manufacturer:	G A Lessner Engineering, Boiler & Iron Works, St. Petersburg , Russia.
Engine: Capacity: Power output: No. of cylinders:	4-stroke, T-head, twin-block side-valve. 4559cc. 32hp / 24 kw at 1200rpm. 4.
Gearbox: Final drive:	4-speed and reverse. Chains and sprockets.
Tyre size:	920 x 120mm beaded edge.
Length: Width overall: Height: Wheelbase: Weight:	With 'double phaëton' body – 4330mm. 1600mm. With hood erected – 2450mm. 3310mm. Ready for the road – 1900kg.
Maximum speed:	65kmh (approximately 40mph).
No. of passengers:	5 including driver.

Amongst the features of the Lessner range of passenger cars were the adherence to chain drive, the flywheel with curved spokes to draw air through the radiator and 'water-cooled' brakes.

The Lessner-90 was similar in appearance to the Lessner-22 and 32, but it was a much larger vehicle, and was unusual for the time in that it had a six-cylinder, twin-block, power unit installed. Some excellent coachwork was applied to the Lessner chassis, and in Plate 16 there is an illustration of a formal limousine body fitted to a Lessner-32 by the St. Petersburg carriage-builder Breitigham.

Some notable users of Lessner passenger cars were the Russian Oil Concessionaires Board of Directors, which bought one for use in Iran in 1906, and the Prime Minister of the Russian Duma, Pyotr Stolypin.

Fig. 36. Line-up of Lessner mail vans at the St. Petersburg post office. (Courtesy N Nemirovich & Izdatelstvo Planeta, Moskva)

Fig. 35. The Lessner mail van with twin-cylinder 8hp engine, 1905.

As mentioned earlier in this narrative, Lessner also produced some commercial vehicles; the fire engine made on the 5-ton chassis in 1904 was probably unique, but in 1907 a 2-ton sided truck model was offered to the Russian public, and this machine is illustrated in Fig. 38. It was a shaft-driven vehicle, unlike other Lessner products, and it had an engine of 15hp. In the following year a van model was added to the range – examples of this unit are depicted in Fig. 39 and in Plate 12; it was designed to carry a payload of 1200kg and was supplied with a smaller power unit of 10hp. This van had a maximum speed of only 20kmh.

Lessner also manufactured the two engines for the Lebaudy type airship, the Kretchet (Falcon) which was completed by the Russian Army Airship Works in 1911. These engines were based upon a Panhard & Levassor design and were of 50hp each; they were water-cooled and weighed 5kg per hp.

Unfortunately, the economic climate that prevailed in Czarist Russia before World War I made motor vehicle building a costly business with uncertain rewards; for example, an unfavourable customs policy that was extant at that time encouraged very low import duties on complete vehicles brought in from abroad, but also imposed exceptionally high tariffs on imported tools, spares, accessories and raw materials! Therefore, even a large enterprise such as Lessner found it difficult to compete with foreign imports, and despite many attempts by the management to interest Russian state organisations without any success whatsoever, it was impossible for them to continue operations, and consequently the motor vehicle division was closed at the end of the 1909 season.

References to Lessner motor vehicles in other literature

Avtomobili Ctrana Sovetov (Automobiles of the Soviet Land) – L. M. Shugurov & V. P. Sirshov, Izdatelstvo Dosaaf, Moscow – 1980(Russian text).

Aviatsiya V Roccii (Aviation in Russia) – M. V. Kellash, G. P. Svishchev & S. A. Khristianov, Izdatelstvo Mashinostroenie, Moscow – 1988, page 264 (Russian text).

Za Rulem (The Helmsman) – Russian motoring magazine, index no. 70321 – 1983.

Avtoexport Round-up, no. 69 – Quarterly trade magazine in English, published by the Russian Trade Organisation V/O Avtoexport, Moscow.

Some brief specifications of the products of this company have been discovered in Russian archives and these are given opposite:

Fig. 37. The Lessner-32 passenger car that was derived from the German, Mercedes range. (Drawing by A Zarakov)

Model	Date	No. cylinders /capacity (cc)	Hp/rpm	No. gears	Wheel diameter	Speed (kmh)
Postal Van	1905-1906	2/1528	8/1000	3	1400mm	30
12hp	1906-1909	2/nk	12/nk	3	-	50
22hp	1907-1909	4/nk	22/nk	4	-	60
32hp	1907-1909	4/4559	32/1200	4	1450mm	65
90hp	1908-1909	6/nk	90/nk	4	1450mm	100
1.2-ton	1908-1909	2/nk	10/nk	3	-	20
2-ton	1907-1909	2/nk	15/nk	4	-	15

Dimensions (where known) of Lessner models			
Model	Wheelbase *	Weight	No. of passengers
Postal Van	1670mm	-	2
12hp	3020mm	-	4-5
22hp	3340mm	-	5-7
32hp	3310mm	1900kg	5-7
90hp	3800mm	-	2-4
1.2-ton	-	1.2-ton (load)	1
2-ton	-	2-ton (load)	2

Notes on above specifications – All Lessner models had
T-head side-valve engines. The 2-ton truck had shaft drive, the
1200kg had chain drive.
* Could be length overall.

Fig. 38. The 2-ton shaft-drive Lessner truck model. (Courtesy V/O Avtoexport)

Fig. 39. The Lessner 1200kg payload motor van of 1908. (Courtesy N Nemirovich & Izdatelstvo Planeta, Moskva)

IX. EMIL LIDTKE, ST. PETERSBURG

This individual was the proprietor of a small bicycle workshop in the capital. Not much has been recorded concerning his exploits, though he has been noted as an 'inventor' in Russian texts. He is known to have produced a small two-seater car in 1901 which had a twin-cylinder engine of 709cc capacity, and a power output of between 3 and 3½hp at 1000rpm. Its main claim to fame was the fact that the car had independent front suspension using transverse leaf springs; however, this feature was not an original one, for Amedée Bollée Père in France had utilised it some twenty years earlier on his La Mancelle steam carriages.

Unfortunately, the author has been unable to discover any illustrations of a Lidtke vehicle.

X. M. A. NAKASHIDZE, WARSAW, POLAND.

This gentleman, a Georgian by birth, was originally an army man, the Commander of the Cossack Group of the Manchurian Army. He is noted as one of the pioneers of the armoured car philosophy, and credited with producing designs for such a vehicle as early as 1904. He put forward his scheme to the Russian Defence Ministry, but, unfortunately, it was rejected. Nevertheless, he sent all of his drawings and relevant data to a French automobile builder who did make a number of vehicles to his designs (see Chapter 4).

Later on Nakashidze set up a workshop in Warsaw, which was in Russian Imperial territory before World War I, where he is recorded as constructing a number of 10-seater hotel buses. These buses were based on an International chassis that was stated to have a four-cylinder, water-cooled 10hp engine and shaft-drive. This was probably the International Harvester J-30 model which was a 'high-wheel' vehicle current in 1911. A search of the archive of the International Harvester Co. of Chicago, Illinois does not reveal any sales of these chassis to Nakashidze, and perhaps he had a licence agreement with the American firm, actually building the whole vehicle in his works.

References to Nakashidze in other literature

Avtoexport Round-up, no. 76 – Russian trade magazine, V/O Avtoexport, Moscow.
Russian Tanks 1900-1970 – John Milsom, Arms & Armour Press, London – 1970.
Tank & Other Armoured Fighting Vehicles – B. T. White, Blandford Press, London – 1970.
Those Wonderful Old Automobiles – Floyd Clymer, McGraw-Hill Book Co. Inc, New York – 1953.

XI. ZAVOD PHOENIX, ST. PETERSBURG

This is another factory about which very little has been recorded. An illustration by Zakarov (Fig. 40), depicts a tractor and semi-trailer outfit manufactured in 1915. The payload was rated at 10 tons and a four-cylinder 60hp engine was fitted. Maximum speed was a mere 15kmh, or 10mph. The vehicle is very reminiscent of the Garford line, an American commercial manufactured by the Garford Motor Truck Co. of Lima, Ohio. These US trucks were exported to Russia prior to World War I, and the Phoenix may have either been a copy or a licence-built version.

XII. RUSSKY AVTOMOBILII ZAVOD I. P. PUZYREVA (RAAIPP), ST. PETERSBURG (RUSSIAN AUTOMOBILE FACTORY .I P. PUZYREV)

Ivan Puzyrev (or Puzyriov as sometimes spelt) was a successful lawyer in St. Petersburg, and extremely interested in the production of an all-Russian motorcar. His brief was that a quality motor vehicle could be produced in the country using only Russian design, labour and raw materials, and in 1909 he set out to put his theories into practice.

A factory was established in St. Petersburg, and at first Puzyrev just sold accessories, later concentrating on repairs, and then manufacturing spare parts. From these activities he gradually accumulated sufficient knowledge to proceed to the production of motorcars designed in-house. Puzyrev investigated the causes of the frequent breakdowns and wear and tear in Russian roads, and he sought to prevent the

consequences of this damage with his second objective, "to develop and build a specifically Russian automobile suitable for transport conditions found in Russia, and for our roads."

With just three employees Ivan Puzyrev commenced production at the end of 1910, and by the following year had made the prototype, designated the 28-35 model. This car was fitted with a double-phaëton open body and it is shown in Fig. 41. Everything was made in the factory except the magneto, carburettor and tyres, whilst the design was totally indigenous. In fact, this car was probably the only Russian motor vehicle which did not owe anything to outside design and technology prior to World War I.

By 1912 the workforce had grown to 98 employees and full-scale production was envisaged. The prototype was uprated to 40hp, and an output of between 8 and 15 cars per annum was predicted. These cars were of simple but rugged design, and featured a four-cylinder, T-head, side-valve engine with two camshafts. Also, Puzyrev patented a four-speed constant mesh gearbox with the various speeds engaged by dog-clutches. This was an innovation, for it may have been the first occasion that such a form of transmission had been utilised. Another feature of these cars was the placement of the controls, gear and brake lever inside the body rather than outside, as was the usual practice at that time. The use of aluminium for the crankcase, the gear casing and the differential housing were forward-looking, as was the use of a fully-floating back axle. The chassis channel frames were stamped out in a local factory (probably the Izhorski or Putilov works), whilst local Treugolnik tyres were fitted. In all probability the magnetos may have been

PHOENIX BOLSTER-TYPE TRUCK.
1915.
CARRYING CAPACITY 10 TONS.
FOUR-CYLINDER, 60 hp ENGINE.
SPEED 15 kph.

Fig. 40. The Phoenix Bolster-type truck of 1915. Carrying capacity 10 tons. Four-cylinder 60hp engine, speed 15kmh. (Courtesy Picture V/O Avtoexport)

Fig. 41. The prototype Puzyrev model 28/35 passenger car.

Fig. 42. The Puzyrev torpedo-bodied A28/40 car of 1912, used for the run from St. Petersburg to Paris and back in 1913. (Courtesy N. Nemirovich & Izdatelstvo Planeta, Moskva)

that the latter model was unique, being shown as a chassis at the 4th International Automobile Exhibition at St. Petersburg in 1913. Two other Puzyrev vehicles were also on display at this motor show; one was an enclosed, formal, limousine and the other was a double-phaëton 7-seater, open tourer (see Plate 13), both of them being mounted on A28-40 chassis.

A high spot for the marque occurred in 1912 when a successful long-distance run from St. Petersburg to Paris and back was accomplished without unwanted stoppages or breakdowns. This run was undertaken by Ivan Puzyrev himself, and it demonstrated the excellent reliability of his cars. The car that was used is depicted in Fig. 41, where it is seen to be an elegant 'torpedo'-bodied sporting model; whether or not it was the A28-40 Sport is, however, open to conjecture. Nevertheless, the A28-40 Sport has a valid claim to fame in that it was the first Russian-built motor vehicle to be fitted with an overhead valve gear. As this 1912 trans-Europe run proved the reliability and the rugged construction of the Puzyrev car, success would be assured.

Once again, though, success eluded an able pioneer due to the Czarist mentality when it came to industrial enterprises. The company did not receive sufficient orders to sustain output, due in part to foreign competition, and Ivan Puzyrev applied for support from the authorities – just as Grigory Lessner had – but received little interest. In Puzyrev's case, the Military High Command did purchase two cars, which was a better result than Lessner's application. These political problems were made even worse when, in January 1914, fire broke out at the factory with devastating results; the main assembly hall was destroyed, together with eight complete cars and fifteen sets of components destined for assembly. After this disaster Puzyrev approached foreign firms for assistance, again without success, and in the autumn of 1914 he died, with his successors moving on to a different line of business.

Between 1911 and 1914 the Russky Automobile Factory I. P. Puzyrev delivered about 40 cars, but unfortunately, none of them have survived to the present day. Apparently the last mention of a Puzyrev car was long ago, in 1923, when an example is reported to have achieved 99kmh in a standing start 1 verst competition in Petrograd (St. Petersburg).

supplied by the Singer Magneto Factory in Podolsk, which left only the carburettor to be sourced from abroad.

The Puzyrev was truly an all-Russian product, from initial design to delivery to the showroom. As there were a number of excellent body builders operating at that time in Imperial Russia, carriage-work would also have been indigenous.

Having built a successful prototype, the Puzyrev firm deemed it prudent to embark upon the manufacture of a range of suitable passenger cars. Three models were offered during the life of the company, and these were the small 23-32 type that was current for only one year (1911-1912), the mainstream type, the A28-40, and the A28-40 Sport; the former was in production from 1912 to 1914, but it is believed

Specifications of cars from the Russky Avtomobili Zavod I. P. Puzyreva

Puzyrev model 23-32, 1911 to 1912

Engine:	Four-cylinder, twin-block, T-head, side valve.
Capacity:	5125cc.
Bhp:	32 at 1200rpm.
Gearbox:	4-speed and reverse, constant mesh.
Final drive:	Shaft.
Wheelbase:	2950mm.
No. of seats:	5.
Max. speed:	70kmh.

Puzyrev model 28-35, 1911 prototype

Engine:	Four-cylinder, twin-block, T-head, side-valve.
Capacity:	5130cc.
Bhp:	35 at 1200rpm.
Gearbox:	3-speed and reverse, constant mesh, with final drive by shaft.
Wheelbase:	3000mm.
Length overall:	4120mm.
Max. speed:	70kmh.

Puzyrev model A28-40, 1912 to 1914

Engine:	Four-cylinder, twin-block, T-head,
Capacity:	side-valve.
Bhp:	6325cc.
Transmission:	40/29 kw at 1200rpm.
	4-speed constant mesh gearbox, cone-clutch and final drive by shaft.
Wheels:	Wooden artillery wheels with security bolts
Tyre size:	1400mm diameter.
	880 x 120mm beaded edge.
Length overall:	4700mm.
Wheelbase:	3320mm.
Weight:	1900kg (all-up) 1860kg (dry).
Suspension:	Semi-elliptical front, C-spring leaf rear.
Lighting:	Acetylene, head and oil side.
No. of seats:	5 to 7.
Max. speed:	90kmh.

Puzyrev Sport

There is some confusion regarding this model. Some references state that it was the A28-40 Sport model, but other sources give the engine capacity as 3929cc. It had a four-speed constant mesh gearbox and shaft drive, was fitted with overhead valve gear, and had seating for two occupants. It was unique, and was not, in all probability, the St. Petersburg-Paris-St. Petersburg car.

References to Puzyrev cars in other literature

Journals:

Avtoexport Round-up, no. 72 – Quarterly journal of the Russian Trade Organisation, V/O Avtoexport, Volkhonka, Moscow.

Puzyrev, no. 6 – A28-40

Za Rulyem, no. 3 – Russian motoring journal, The Collection, 1983.

Za Rulyem – 29th April 1985, "Zavod Puzyreva and its Automobiles," D. Kozlov, Assistant, Automobile Department of the Polytechnical Museum of the USSR, Moscow.

XIII. I. V. ROMANOV, ELECTRICAL ENGINEER, ST. PETERSBURG

Ippolit Romanov was an enthusiast for electric traction on the highway and during the first decade of the 20th century he sought to place a service of battery-electric omnibuses on the streets of St. Petersburg; he also built some electrically propelled hansom-type cabs that were fitted with rear steering.

Romanov started work in 1899, and by the following year he had staged the first public demonstration of urban electric vehicles in St. Petersburg. This demonstration featured two taxi-cabs, which are illustrated in Plate 1. One of these cabs had an open fronted 'Victoria' style of body, whilst the other was fitted with a 'half-coach' or 'coupé' style, being enclosed and having a large area of glass in the passenger compartment. The drivers of these vehicles sat high up at the rear of the body in the way hansom cabs were driven, and the power was taken by the front wheels with the steering at the rear; the bodies of these cabs were manufactured by Messrs Freze of St. Petersburg, and were of the highest quality. Each driving wheel had its own electric motor in order to obviate the use of a differential, and the battery capacity, which accounted for 48 per cent of the total weight of the vehicle, had a range of 64km.

The batteries were stored in a box beneath the driver's seat. These cabs had a maximum speed of 38kmh, which is about 22mph, and with their large diameter artillery wheels shod with solid rubber tyres, their silence in operation, and their plush leather seating, they were said to have been extremely comfortable. Bells were fitted by the front step, and these must have constantly rung whilst the cab progressed.

Following the success with the taxi-cabs, Romanov produced his omnibus version and placed it in service in February 1901. Presumably he built others to provide a proper network, but there was, unfortunately, constant opposition from the tramway enterprise and the proprietors of horse-drawn cabs, so much so that the city fathers of St. Petersburg appeared to have had no option but to terminate the use of the electric buses.

Romanov's omnibuses were elegant vehicles (Fig. 43), with an 8-light body, four each side, the middle two being able to slide halfway. A rear platform was fitted to allow, perhaps, two or three standing passengers, whilst the saloon accommodated

Fig. 43. I. Romanov's Electric Omnibus, used in St. Petersburg in 1901. (Drawing by A Zakarov)

XIV. IVAN YUSHKOV

As was the case in other countries, Russia was also involved in the 'cycle car' craze, and the first of these to appear was a very skimpy two seater vehicle with the seats set in tandem; it was made as a prototype in 1915 by Ivan Yushkov. This engineer probably worked in St. Petersburg, but the writer has been unable to determine accurately where his workshop was located.

The car, which is illustrated in Plate 9, was typical of its genre, having a wooden chassis and body, a twin-cylinder motorcycle engine (probably of Harley-Davidson origin), a friction variable speed transmission system, and final drive by pulleys and belts. The primitive wire and bobbin steering turned the centre pivoted front axle. All in all, this vehicle was a crude affair built very much along the lines of the English Carden and A. V. Monocar efforts of the 1920s. Another similar, three-wheeled cycle car named the OKTA was made in Soviet times, in 1933, and this was fitted with an 8hp, 469cc engine that gave it a maximum speed of 60kmh, or about 36mph. Unfortunately, the maker of this creation remains un-recorded. (Fig. 44) This style of vehicle was lightweight, weighing around just 300kg, their construction was flimsy and their currency remained short. The car made by Yushkov was never put into production, as it appeared just before the onset of war in Russia in 1915.

Apart from the fourteen builders mentioned in detail in the foregoing text, there were a number of other firms and individuals involved in the motor industry in Russia during Czarist times, but of which little has been recorded. Pyotr Freze (see section IV) is known to have made an experimental trolley bus, whilst the D. Skavronsky Machine Tool Factory in St. Petersburg is reputed to have made a passenger car with electric lighting in 1903. Yevgeny Yakovlev, who collaborated with Freze to make the first Russian motorcar, never made another one, but concentrated on stationary engines, whilst individuals named as Krushchev and Shidlovsky are said to have one car each prior to 1914. A person recorded as Potrovsky made a surface carburettor in 1894, whilst I. Romanov had mastered the art of battery-electric transmission by 1899.

a further 17 people. Again, large diameter artillery wheels with solid rubber tyres were fitted, and the motors drove the rear pair independently using a belt drive system. Electric lighting was provided, whilst the bodies were made from a special form of panel made by laminating several layers of fabric and plywood impregnated with glue and subjected to high temperatures and pressures. This made the whole vehicle quite light, weighing just 1600kg.

Some specifications of these omnibuses have been recorded as follows:

Length overall:	3500mm.
Width overall:	2000mm.
Height to top of clerestory:	2700mm.
Wheelbase:	2650mm.
Weight all up:	1600kg.
Motor:	Each one 6hp/4.5 kw at 1800rpm. Range 60km.
Speed range:	11-19kmh.

References to Romanov in other literature
Avtoexport Round-up, nos. 68 & 76.
Za Rulyem no. 1 – 1985.

Plate 13. Puzyrev motor vehicles.

THE PROTOTYPE OF THE
28-35 MODEL BUILT IN 1911.
DISPLACEMENT OF THE
FOUR-CYLINDER ENGINE—5,130 cc,
POWER—35 hp AT 1,200 rpm,
WHEELBASE—3,000 mm.

THE PUZYRIOV-A28-40 CAR BUILT
IN 1912 (6,325 cc, 40 hp) WITH A
FIVE-SEAT TORPEDO BODY ON A
3,320 mm WHEELBASE CHASSIS.
THIS CAR TRAVELLED FROM
ST. PETERSBURG TO PARIS AND BACK.

Русскій Автомобильный Заводъ
И. П. ПУЗЫРЕВЪ.
С.-ПЕТЕРБУРГЪ.

THE PUZYRIOV-A28-40 CAR BUILT
IN 1913 WITH A
SEVEN-SEAT OPEN BODY. IT
HAD A FOUR-CYLINDER,
6,325 cc, 40 hp (AT 1,200 rpm)
ENGINE, AND A WHEELBASE OF
3,320 mm.

3. PRE-REVOLUTIONARY COACHBUILDERS

There were ten, or perhaps more, specialist carriage builders operating in Russia prior to the outbreak of World War I and the ensuing Revolution in 1917, and all of these enterprises produced exceptional work on both domestic and foreign chassis. In its homeland, Russian coachwork was always adjudged to be superior to foreign bodywork, because it had to be made to a higher standard of construction to cope with the bad conditions found on the local roads at that time; unfortunately, the best of carriage-work from overseas, even that from such esteemed names as Kellner and Castagna, was prone to shake itself to pieces in a short space of time due to those atrocious roads. However, many importers of foreign marques did specify to manufacturers that strengthened chassis and enhanced bodywork should be applied to all vehicles sold in Russia.

Curiously, the Russians had a preference for French products, and most imported makes were of French origin, as were the majority of aircraft used during World War I. For example, Messrs Peugeot advertised in the Moscow motoring journal *The Automobilist*, just before the war, that its cars were "Luxury Automobiles for Russian Roads"; this firm was also very well represented all over the country, with a head office in St. Petersburg at Kamenoostrorovskier Ploshad (Square), Kronverksnaya St. nos. 2-13, and a number of repair depots in other cities including Moscow, Kiev, Kharkov, Ekaterinoslav, Rostov, Odessa and Warsaw. Another French firm, Messrs Brasier, also advertised in the same magazine in 1913, giving an address in Moscow at Karetnii Row, property no. 4. Local organizations became specialist representatives as well, with S. N. Baykov at B. Sadobaya No. 14, Moscow selling Minerva cars and emphasising its Knight 'patent engine' as having no valves. Another company, T-vo B Reshetilov & Co., also situated at Kamenoostrorovskier Ploshad in St. Petersburg (no. 19), enthused about the

Plate 14. Russian coachbuilders in Czarist times – Pyotr Ilyin's creations.

Knight engine in its 1915 advert, in the Moscow journal referring to the British Daimler car. Other agents in Russia selling foreign makes included G. A. Lessner, which imported Mercedes vehicles, and P. Ilyin, which extolled the virtue of the French La Buire range of motorcars.

Some details of the more outstanding Russian coachbuilders are given here:

MOSCOW LTD. CO., AUTOMOBILE EQUIPMENT FACTORY, PYOTR ILYIN MOSCOW, KARETNII ROW, PROPERTY NO. 43.

This prominent Russian firm commenced business in 1805, and over the years gained an excellent reputation for its wares, which included ordinary carts and wagons, as well as carriages and road coaches for wealthy patrons.

In 1904, Pyotr Ilyin, who headed the firm at the time,

Fig. 44. The 3-wheeled Okta cycle car of 1933.

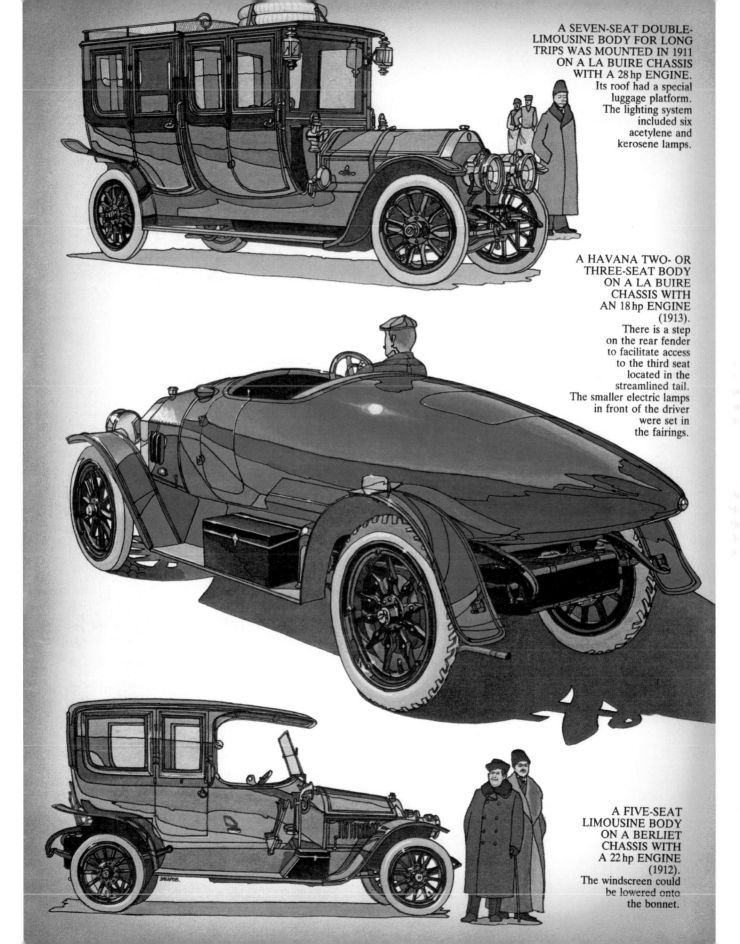

A SEVEN-SEAT DOUBLE-LIMOUSINE BODY FOR LONG TRIPS WAS MOUNTED IN 1911 ON A LA BUIRE CHASSIS WITH A 28 hp ENGINE. Its roof had a special luggage platform. The lighting system included six acetylene and kerosene lamps.

A HAVANA TWO- OR THREE-SEAT BODY ON A LA BUIRE CHASSIS WITH AN 18 hp ENGINE (1913). There is a step on the rear fender to facilitate access to the third seat located in the streamlined tail. The smaller electric lamps in front of the driver were set in the fairings.

A FIVE-SEAT LIMOUSINE BODY ON A BERLIET CHASSIS WITH A 22 hp ENGINE (1912). The windscreen could be lowered onto the bonnet.

Moscow Limited Company
Automobile equipment factory. P. Ilyin.
Moscow Karetnii Row, property no. 43.
Address for telegrams: Moscow Autogarage.

Telephone: Out of hours 31-41.
Factory 305-41.
Garage 238-20.

Top of the range Limousine 'Demi-Ronde'

DEPARTMENT	DEPARTMENT	DEPARTMENT
Automobile Repair	Body Building	Automobile Parts

Michelin tyres, lamps, loud hailers, horns, sirens.
Best prices for all automobile components.

Fig. 45. Advertisement for the coachbuilder P. Ilyin, with translation.

branched out into the motorcar business, becoming an agent for several foreign manufacturers including Delage, Dürkopp, Panhard & Levassor, Humber, and more importantly, La Buire. At this time, Ilyin opened his repair workshops, after entering into an agreement with Messrs Chantiers de la Buire of Lyons to assemble its cars under licence from imported components. La Buire was to make a multiplicity of models up to 1914, but Ilyin confined himself mainly to the 28/35 model. By 1912 Ilyin was making many of the parts himself, and the car eventually became known as the Russky-Buire. This car had a 4-cylinder, side-valve, 4074cc engine, a wheelbase of 3080mm, wheel diameter of 1450mm, seating for between 5 and 7 persons, and, in tourer standard form, a dry weight of 1820kg. When carrying enclosed formal coachwork the car was capable of a maximum speed of about 60/70kmh.

The Ilyin enterprise quickly became the premier coach-building firm in Imperial Russia, and at the height of its fame for its coachwork it was completing between 40 and 50 custom-made car bodies of the finest quality per annum. In 1911, Pyotr

Ilyin himself entered a self-prepared vehicle in the St. Petersburg to Sevastopol Rally, completing the distance without any fault occurring, thus demonstrating the expertise that prevailed in his factory. By 1912, *The Automobilist* had stated that the plant was capable of producing coachwork "... satisfying every wish of the customer as regards shape and finish and meeting the requirements of Russian roads and climate in both materials and craftsmanship"; also in 1912, Ilyin relinquished his other agencies to concentrate upon the production of La Buire chassis and to provide specialist carriage-work that included formal limousines, landaulettes, 'torpedo' tourers, and coupes etc., together with commercial van, omnibus and truck bodies. In this latter activity, his van bodies were supreme.

Between 1911 and 1912 the works were expanded to include a large concrete assembly hall that provided accommodation for about 150 vehicles under construction. By this time Ilyin's facility had evolved into a proper manufacturing venue, incorporating a machine shop, wood-working shop, panel beating/body shops, a trimming shop and so on. The only

Konstantin
Shaparov.

Fig. 46. Two of the NAMI-1 prototypes about to start on the test run from Moscow to Leningrad.
(Picture Za Rulyem)

problem with the Karetnii Row area, where a number of garage enterprises were housed, was that access was rather constrained due to the closeness of other buildings.

A highlight of the Ilyin saga was his success in the 4th International Automobile Exhibition at St. Petersburg in 1913, where he placed four vehicles on show. There was a massive enclosed, formal limousine mounted on a 28/40hp, 5346cc chassis and a streamlined Havana sports two-seater on an 18hp, 2305cc chassis, both of which were of La Buire origin, a 6-seater 'Torpedo' tourer on a Fiat 28/35hp chassis, and a special ambulance of in-house design that was said to have been fitted with a La Buire model 200-A two-stroke engine. The RIAS house journal *Avtomobil*, edited by A Nagel no less, remarked on the prowess of Ilyin at the exhibition as follows:

"Ilyin's car bodies matched the best foreign-made ones in every respect. The limousine had suede leather, light grey upholstery; the interior included gilded instruments, pear-wood inlay, dome lights, glove-compartments, porte-boquets and other luxury fittings. The attractive and smooth body lines combined with exquisite and lasting finish confirm that Russia can produce automobile bodies as good as any made abroad."

The ambulance shown was highly regarded and was awarded the Grand Gold Medal at the exhibition. It is on record that Ilyin's factory employed the best craftsmen available, utilised the best techniques of the age, and that he fitted up all of the wooden parts of the carriage-work without nails or screws, using only shaped parts and dowels glued together; interior panels were made from hardwood ply covered in best grained leather or quality fabrics, with the exterior of the body panels

having between 18 and 20 coats of paint finished off with a coat of copal lacquer. Drying and polishing between coats took many days until surfaces achieved a mirror-like gleam. Pyotr Ilyin was an excellent engineer, and he surrounded himself with employees with similar skills.

In 1912, Ilyin supplied the Russian Ministry of Defence with a Russo-Buire 6-seater touring car for tests to determine its suitability as a staff car, but the outcome of these trials is unclear. During World War I the firm built a batch of 150hp Sunbeam Cossack aero-engines, which were mainly used in Igor Sikorsky's four-engined Ilya Mourometz aircraft instead of the German Argus units, which were no longer available. Also, the Russian Army was supplied with ambulances from Ilyin's works.

By the end of World War I, and in the aftermath of the Bolshevik Revolution, Pyotr Ilyin's plant was taken over by the Soviets, primarily as an automobile repair shop; however, they retained Ilyin as the Technical Director, and it seems that he continued to supervise work there until the factory was incorporated into the large AMO Works in Moscow (Avtomobil Moskva Obschenii), or Moscow Automobile Association, later on to become the ZIS (Zavod imeni Stalina) and finally the ZIL (Zavod imeni Likhachev). Ilyin's enterprise was renamed the Spartak Zavod and at first, during the early 1920s, it was used to facilitate running repairs to motor vehicles, to continue the production of specialist bodywork, and to manufacture a small pedestrian controlled two-wheeled tractor for small-holdings. The main claim to fame of the Spartak Works was that it was the venue for the first indigenous Soviet motorcar design, the NAMI, and details of this venture are included in this narrative as it follows on directly from Pyotr Ilyin's stewardship.

Fig. 47. Drawing of the NAMI-1 1928 production vehicle.

As has been discussed previously in this narrative, during the first ten years of Soviet rule following the 1917 October Revolution there was little production of any type of motor vehicle, let alone private motorcars. There was, of course, the Prombron – a resuscitated form of Russo-Balt, manufactured in very small quantities in 1922-23, with some passenger bodies fitted to the light truck chassis – and the AMO-F-15, which was made in Moscow from 1924 onwards; both of these models were derived from other, foreign designs, and therefore could not be considered as 'original' designs. However, in 1925 moves towards general industrialisation were being made by the Politburo under the direction of Josef Stalin, with the formulation of the first five-year plan; amongst the proposals for this plan were provisions for passenger car manufacture in the USSR.

There was, at the time, a 26 year old engineering graduate from Moscow named Konstantin Shaparov, who had produced some designs for a novel economy car that appeared to have some merit, and consequently he was invited to take up a post at the Nauchnii Avto-Motornii Institut (Scientific Automobile & Motor Institute) located in the capital.

Shaparov teamed up with two other men, Andrei Lipgart and Eugenii Charnko, and began building the first prototype at the Institute; Andrei Lipgart was later to become well known as the designer of the GAZ-20 Pobeda, the first totally new design of passenger car to be manufactured in any country after World War II. This prototype, or 'pilot model' as the Russians styled it, was given the title of NAMI-1 (НАМИ-1), a designation that was eventually transferred to the whole of the production series. The first example was completed by May Day 1927 (see Fig. 47), and two more experimental versions were finished in the following September; these three cars all had rounded grilles and bonnets, with the production models having pointed grille surrounds.

The two later prototypes had different body styles, one being a two-seat roadster and the other a four-seat tourer (see illustration at the top of Plate 15); both of these models were subjected to extended tests over difficult terrain to evaluate their suitability for Russian conditions. In the photograph (Fig. 46) the two vehicles are shown at the start of the Moscow-Leningrad-Moscow run, which was carried out in gruelling and adverse circumstances in the winter of 1927/1928. Other runs such as the Moscow-Tibilsi-Kraym and back were also undertaken, and the cars gave a creditable performance by completing journeys of over 1500 kilometres on earth roads, cobble stones and rough tracks, for there were few paved roads in the USSR outside of the towns at that time. Following the completion of these trials the design was accepted for production in 1928.

The NAMI-1 was in production for three years during which time some 269 units were made including the three prototypes; 3 were manufactured in 1927, 50 in 1928, 156 in 1929 and 160 in 1930. Although the above output figures were verified by the Polytechnical Museum of the USSR, there is some confusion concerning the actual number of units constructed, for the final chassis number in 1930 is quoted as no. 375.

The basic design of the NAMI-1 was both unconventional and interesting, for it employed ideas that were in advance of its time, and which deviated from normal or accepted practice. The car was built around a tubular backbone with a diameter of 135mm, which supported the Vee-twin, air-cooled engine at the front and the three-speed gearbox at the rear. The propellor shaft ran down the centre of this chassis tube. The power unit had a capacity of 1160cc and in its original form developed 18.5bhp at

2800rpm. The suspension system was by means of a beam axle at the front with quarter-elliptical leaf springs, and by a swing axle and a transverse leaf spring at the rear. The four-seater body was attached to the chassis frame at four points and it was of extremely simple construction, with only two doors: one on the left at the front and the other on the right at the rear. Again, for the sake of simplicity, no differential was fitted, which allowed better traction on bad terrain and snow, though at the expense of considerable tyre wear. This feature, coupled with a high ground clearance of 225mm, gave the vehicle good off-road performance.

The weight of the NAMI-1 was 700kg in standard form with the four-seater body, with the solitary roadster tipping the scales at 622kg. The wheelbase was 2800mm and the track 1200mm. Maximum speed was quoted as between 70 and 75kmh, or about 45mph, with fuel consumption 9/10 litres per 100 kilometres, or around 30mpg. The fuel was contained in a dashboard-mounted gravity tank whose filler cap was sited in the centre of the scuttle.

Altogether the NAMI-1 was a pleasing light car in aspect, though, to some tastes, it would appear stark and austere. However, the whole of the body design was of elegant plainness with no factory or other emblems adorning any part of it; the only plated parts to be seen on the body were the door handles, the filler cap and the headlamp bezels. A quaint reminder of early days on the continent was the retention of right-hand drive; the reason given for this archaic feature in a country which drove on the right-hand side of the road was that, as the cities of the Soviet Union were always crowded with pedestrians, horse-carts, hand barrows and bicycles, which always appeared suddenly on the driver's nearside, it was prudent to have the driving position there as well! Luckily, four of these cars survive to the present day, one having been found in daily use in the city of Irkutsk in 1970. This is Chassis No. 107, and it has been restored to its original condition and is now an exhibit in the NAMI Museum in Moscow; it is often brought out for various shows and trade fairs and still runs well under its own power. Another similar example is displayed in the vehicle collection of the Polytechnical Museum in Moscow.

In 1932 Konstantin Shaparov developed the NAMI-1 into a more sophisticated vehicle named the NATI-2 (НАТИ-2), but this was a purely experimental exercise done under the aegis of another organization, the Nauchnii Avto-Traktornii Institut (Scientific Auto-Tractor Institute), which has now been absorbed into NAMI. The NATI-2 was directly derived from the Vee-twin NAMI-1, having the same tubular backbone chassis layout, but with a four-cylinder engine and more elaborate bodywork.

Two different, ducted, fan-cooled four-cylinder engines were used in the NATI-2, with a side-valve version being installed in a four-seater tourer and a station wagon, and an ohv unit fitted to a roadster-bodied variant. Both types of power unit had a swept volume of 1211cc and bore and stroke measurements of 62mm x 100mm; the side-valve type produced 22bhp at 2800rpm, whilst the ohv engine provided an extra 2bhp at the same rotational engine speed. Although the NATI-2 was heavier than its predecessor at between 720 and 730kg, according to

the body style fitted, it returned a better fuel consumption of 32mpg, though maximum speed was about the same as that of the NAMI-1. The four-seat tourer and the station wagon had a wheelbase of 2730mm, whilst the roadster measured 2430mm; the track remained the same at 1200mm on all models.

The illustration of the NATI-2 (Plate 15) clearly depicts the more luxurious styling of this car with its electro-plated 'radiator' surround, windshield frame, double bumper and headlights, and the use of wire wheels in place of the pressed steel ones on the previous production series. Also shown is the changeover to left-hand drive (the chassis drawing shows the NATI-2 in right-hand drive form.) Once again this Soviet light car design was a pleasing vehicle to observe, and it is a pity that it was not put into production to found a base for original Soviet automotive thinking and design in the 1930s.

The demise of the NAMI-1 and abandonment of the NATI-2 project were due to two main factors: one was that the Spartak Works, situated in the old part of Moscow, was hemmed in by large apartment buildings and had poor access and no room for expansion, and the other was that the Soviet trading organisation Amtorg signed a multimillion dollar deal with Henry Ford to erect a carbon copy of the Baton Rouge plant at Nizhny Novgorod, to manufacture Ford model A tourers and model AA trucks in large volume. These reasons effectively killed off the NAMI/NATI project after the four final NATI-2 prototypes were finished in 1932. By the end of 1932, the Gorky Automobilove Zavod was in full swing making Ford vehicles by the thousand, and thoughts about original Russian design were lost.

Specifications for the NAMI-1 Phaëton – 1927 to 1930	
Manufacturer:	Spartak Works, Moscow.
Engine: Bore: Stroke: Bhp: Torque: Capacity: Valve-gear:	Air-cooled, twin-cylinder in Vee formation. 84mm. 105mm. 18.5 at 2600rpm (later 22 at 2800rpm). 5.5kg/meter at 2200rpm. 1160cc. ohv.
Gearbox:	3-speed mounted at rear of chassis.
Weight (dry): Wheelbase: Track:	750kg. 2800mm. 1200mm (front and rear).
Maximum speed: Fuel consumption:	75kmh 10 litres per 100km.
No. of seats:	4.

NB: The NATI-2 has a 4-cylinder engine, with a bore and stroke of 98.43mm x 107.95mm and torque of 5.6kg/m at 2200rpm.

BIBLIOGRAPHY

Avtoexport Round-up, Soviet trade magazine.
Automobilia Vestures Lappuses (History of the Automobile),
    E. Leipins, Zinatne Riga – 1983 (Latvian text).
Kratkii Avtomobilnay Spravochnik (Automobile Specification
    Book), Avtransizdat, Moscow – 1963 (Russian text).
Ot Russo-Balt do Kamaza (From Russo-Balt to Kamaz), B. I.
    Pustovalov, Vasheishaya Shkola, Minsk – 1984 (Russian text).
Ot Samobegloii Kolyaski do Zil-111 (Early Days to ZIL-111),
    A. S. Isaev, Moskobskii Rabochii, Moscow – 1961 (Russian text).
Za Rulyem (The Driver), Soviet motoring magazine (Russian
    text).

All illustrations in this section were supplied by V/O Avtoexport, Volkhonka St, Moscow.

OTHER NOTABLE CARRIAGE–BUILDERS IN THE CZARIST PERIOD

As well as P. Ilyin, who reached the pinnacle of carriage-building expertise on motor vehicles up to the outbreak of World War I in 1914, there were a number of other factories operating in this field that appear to have had equal capabilities, and that supplied bodies on the chassis of the world's top manufacturers. As has been mentioned elsewhere in this narrative, Russian carriage-work had to be made to much more generous scantlings than those to which other European makers were accustomed, as road surfaces were poor, or often just unmade tracks, whilst body loadings were much greater. Therefore, Russian bodywork had to be sturdy and durable.

On the boundary of the 19th and the 20th centuries, Imperial Russia did have a pool of excellent coachbuilders, some of whom had commenced business in the 1700s, and who had supplied a wealthy clientele with a selection of elegant vehicles including road coaches, phaëtons, barouches, landaus and Victorias etc. These firms also specialised in the production of highly ornamented horse-drawn sledges for use in winter conditions. Some of the more prominent of these manufacturers are discussed here ...

Ivan Breitigham of St. Petersburg was founded in 1864, making bodies for motorcars from 1904 until 1915; the company specialised in furnishing carriage-work on Mercedes and Lessner chassis. It exhibited its wares at the leading shows in Russia, and at the time of the 4th International Automobile Exhibition held in St. Petersburg in 1913, the technical press of the day had this to say about it: "Coachwork from the Russian carriage building factory of Breitigham took one of the prominent places. Vehicles were distinguished by both gracefulness of form and finish, and by strength and beauty of make-up."

P Freze of St. Petersburg was, as has already been noted, a pioneer of motor vehicle construction in Imperial Russia. However, he was also a well-known coachbuilder working from 1896 until about 1907. Freze had made the bodies for Romanov's electric vehicles, and developed a form of glued laminated panel for their interiors, and he had also made all of the bodywork for his own machines. Freze was noted for

a special ambulance body fitted to a Renault chassis that was displayed at the 1st International Automobile Exhibition in St. Petersburg in 1907. This body had some novel features, one of which was the way the stretchers were mounted on the bulkhead behind the driver, rolling outwards when lowered to ensure a quick engagement to receive the patients; folding footboards and an extension canopy were also fitted.

Krummel, also from St. Petersburg, worked from 1906 until 1915, and it specialised in fitting bodies to Hotchkiss chassis.

Another St. Petersburg carriage-works was the Zavod Pobeda (Victory), which possessed a plant with a floor area of 9000 square metres, and it concentrated its efforts on providing the bodies for the Scottish Argyll and the German Opel cars.

Probably the oldest carriage-works in Russia that was making bodywork for motor vehicles was that of P. D. Yakovlev, who commenced business in 1790. Apparently his company's fame had spread all over Europe, as medals had been awarded to its carriages at exhibitions in London (1851), Vienna (1873), and Paris in 1878. Yakovlev began car body construction in 1904 with 180 skilled workers.

All of these enterprises utilised only the best materials available, selecting the best fabrics for the interiors and the finest supple leather for the seating, and supplying instruments with silver bezels, silver plated door handles, and ivory for knobs. Cut-glass flower vases (porte-boquets), drink decanters and glasses were also included.

Of all these carriage-builders, it was probably Breitigham with 400 employees, Yakovlev with 180 and Pobeda with a large assembly area that were the greatest; some of their efforts are illustrated in Plate 16.

The more important carriage-builders	
St. Petersburg	
Breitigham	(400 employees)
Freze & Co.	1896-1906
Krummel	1906-1915
Otto	1915-1917
Pobeda Zavod	1905-1912
P. D. Yakovlev & Co.	1790-1911 (180 employees)
Moscow	
Evseev	1913-1914
P. Ilyin & Co. Ltd.	1805-1918 (continued as Spartak Works until 1932)
Krylov Brothers	1911-1914
Odessa	
Empede	1912-1914

Plate 15 (right). The Soviet NAMI-1 and NATI-2 light cars.

Plate 16 (overleaf). Russian coachbuilders in Czarist times – Breitigham, Freze, Pobeda & Yakovlev.

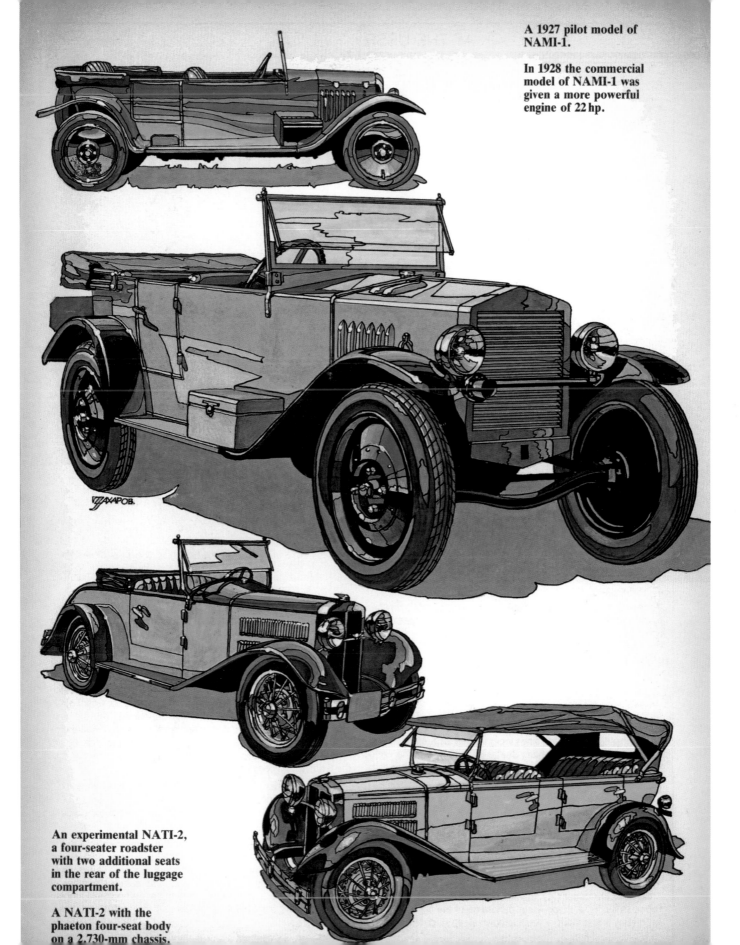

A 1927 pilot model of NAMI-1.

In 1928 the commercial model of NAMI-1 was given a more powerful engine of 22 hp.

An experimental NATI-2, a four-seater roadster with two additional seats in the rear of the luggage compartment.

A NATI-2 with the phaeton four-seat body on a 2,730-mm chassis.

The phaeton body of the Freze
firm on the chassis
of a German car
with a 24-hp engine (1905).

The limousine body made
by the Yakovlev firm
on a Brasier chassis (1907).

The limousine body made
by the Breitiham firm
on a chassis manufactured
at the Lessner plant in
Russia and featuring a 32-hp
engine (1907).

The landaulet body made
by the Pobeda firm
on an Opel chassis
with a 24-hp engine (1912).

4. TRACKED & MILITARY VEHICLES

A number of interesting tracked and military vehicles were produced in Russia up to the end of World War I and into the dawn of the Soviet era. A lightweight form of half-tracked vehicle was developed in Imperial days and this became an important invention particularly in the military sphere of operations.

ADOLPHE KÉGRESSE AND THE DEVELOPMENT OF THE 'AUTO—SLEDGE'

One of the most important inventions in motor vehicle technology was made by a Frenchman named Adolphe Kégresse, who was in charge of the Court Garage of Czar Nicholas II at the Imperial Palace at Tsarskoe Selo, near St. Petersburg. Kégresse had worked at the garage since 1904 and during the time spent there he had always had an interest in developing a reliable cross-country vehicle that would be capable of traversing difficult terrain as well as snow and ice. Apparently he was unhappy witnessing the struggles of horses when they left paved roads to haul sledges over open country during winter, and he resolved to improve the capability of motor vehicles to obviate the misery of these animals.

He devised 'elastic tracks' in 1910, and fitted up a Lessner-Mercedes 32/45hp passenger car with an improvised version of his system as an experiment. Using this car as a basis between 1910 and 1913, Kégresse utilised a number of different materials to ascertain some suitable for traction purposes in the cross-country mode, and these included camel's wool, leather, and finally, rubber; various combinations of sprockets and jockey wheels together with tensioning devices were tried out at the rear of the vehicle, whilst an arrangement of hinged skis was located beneath the front wheels to produce what was the first ATV (All-Terrain Vehicle). Of course, many other inventors had previously produced successful tracklaying systems, mostly for use in the farming industry; one of the first such ideas had been patented by Sir George Cayley in 1825. (British patent no. 5260 of 1825, "New locomotive apparatus for propelling carriages.") This notwithstanding, there was other art prior to the Kégresse invention, when Alvin Oliver Lombard proposed a half-tracked system that was applied to the Lombard Steam Log Hauler, subsequently patented by him on 4th May 1901. (US patent no. 674737 of 1901.) However, Lombard's application was a very heavy-duty chain driven system that would not have been at all suitable for passenger cars and, therefore, Adolphe Kégresse

did have original thought on his side and managed to file a specification in France on 28th February 1913, in the Office National de la Propriété Industrielle. (Brevet d'Inv. no. 454881, sealed on 7th May 1913.) The writer considers that M. Kégresse was fortunate, for in Lombard's specification it was stated that his system could be "... practically adapted to automobiles especially for snow roads."

It seems that Kégresse did not have any problems with his specification for, as far as the writer knows, no-one ever challenged it in law, as was the case with Benjamin Holt in America. Also, the Kégresse système was devised principally for light machines, although it was fitted to armoured cars later on; it differed to the heavier Lombard system in that it was suited to running at speed on paved roads without damage to the surface due to its rubber tracks. These special tracks were developed in collaboration with the Treugolnik Tyre Factory of St. Petersburg, and the outcome was a commercially satisfactory method of transmission, tested with great success on the prototype on the snow-covered ice of the Neva River in the winter of 1913, achieving a maximum speed of 60kmh. As his patent was sealed on 7th May 1913, Kégresse considered it prudent to show off his invention at the 4th International Automobile Exhibition, which occurred at the end of that month; he displayed two examples of his work on Stand No. 152. These vehicles were designated as 'Avto-Sani', or 'Auto-Sledges', and one of them was the prototype from the Russo-Baltic factory in Riga.

During the process of research and development of the Kégresse half-track système, some interaction with the Treugolnik Tyre Factory in St. Petersburg was maintained, with that firm eventually making the rubber tracks on a commercial basis. Initially, the Russo-Baltic plant manufactured the mechanical parts, such as rollers, chainwheels, jockey-wheels and other steel work, but later on this activity was transferred to the Putilov Zavod when the exigencies of war demanded a strengthened version for armoured cars. Apart from the production models, several motorcars were converted to the Kégresse système; these included a Packard Twin-Six for Czar Nicholas II, which is shown in Fig. 46 on Revolution Day in 1917, and a Rolls-Royce 40/50hp Silver Ghost, believed to be Chassis No. 66200 of 1916, which was converted in 1919 for the use of Vladimir Illych Lenin until his death in 1924. This latter car still exists and it was displayed in the Central V. I. Lenin Museum in Soviet days. It is illustrated in Fig. 50 and Plate 17.

The Russo-Balt-S24-35 (1915) had a rubber track and could tow a loaded trailer.

The very first, 1910 design involving the Lessner-Mercèdes chassis. The track was covered with camel wool.

The Rolls-Royce with tracks designed by Kégresse (1916) which was used by V. I. Lenin between 1919 and 1923.

A commercially produced half-track model: the ZIS-42M (1944) with an 85 hp engine.

Plate 17. Half-tracked vehicles – Kégresse and
Soviet style ZIS-42M.

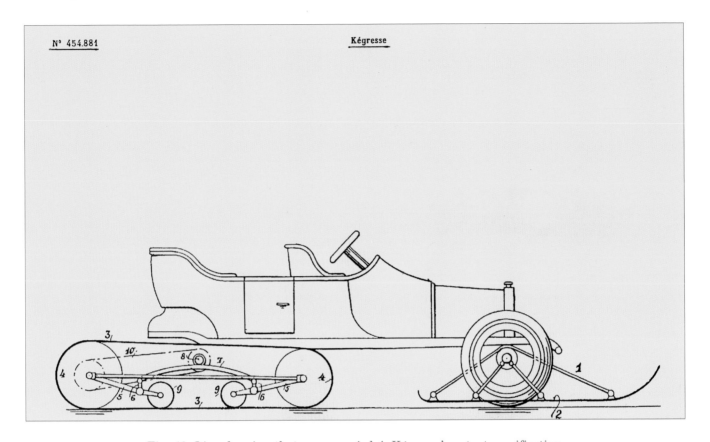

Fig. 48. Line drawing that accompanied A Kégresse's patent specification.

In 1916, Adolphe Kégresse teamed up with an engineer from the Putilov Zavod named Alexei Elizarov to produce military vehicles for the war effort, based upon the Kégresse système. In England, the Austin Motor Co. of Longbridge had produced a 3½-ton truck in 1914, which had the peculiarity of twin propeller shafts. Most of this output was supplied for defence purposes, and some of the vehicles found their way to Russia. A prototype version fitted up with the half-track attachment was tested in the autumn of 1916 on a run from St. Petersburg to Gomel and back, and it was found to be fit for military use. On these trials a maximum speed of 40kmh was attained on paved roadways, but only 9 or 10kmh could be maintained in cross-country mode. The half-track arrangement applied to these Austin trucks and armoured cars was of a heavier pattern than those used on ordinary passenger cars, and eventually the Putilov Zavod manufactured 182 sets of them, of which 60 were applied to the Austin armoured vehicles.

Kégresse left Russia in 1917 to live in France, where his système was successfully exploited by Citroën in its spectacular Trans-Sahara runs of the early 1920s. The outcome of these

African forays was that military authorities in Western Europe became interested in the Kégresse système for field use. In 1923 a Schneider-Citroën armoured car was built (Fig. 49), whilst in England, Messrs. Crossley Motor Co. and H. G. Burford & Co. Ltd. both took up licences for manufacture. Roadless Traction also used it as a basis for its own system, which used the rear axle of the donor vehicle to drive the rear sprocket.

In Fig. 48, the drawing that accompanied the patent specification is illustrated. In this drawing the method of operation of the Kégresse système is clearly depicted. Points 1 and 2 show the method of attaching the skis to the front wheels, 3 is the rubber track, 4 the driven and idler road wheels, 5 the radius arms linking the road wheel spindles to the jockey wheel pins, 9, with 6 and 7 being the balance beam arrangement, 8 the chaindrive sprocket, and 10 the chaindrive itself.

The pioneering work of Kégresse was carried on in Soviet Russia after the inventor left for France in 1917, when two engineers named Alexandr Kuzin and Grigory Sonkin developed a half-track vehicle at the NATI Laboratory (Nauchnii Avto-Traktor Institut). This vehicle, designated the

1917г.
Дни революции.
Автомобиль-Сани диктатора Николая II.

"Revolution Day" Auto-Sledge belonging to the Late Nicholas

Fig. 49. The Packard tourer converted by Adolphe Kégresse for Czar Nicholas II. (Author's collection)

Fig. 50. The Rolls-Royce Silver Ghost belonging to Vladimir Lenin, after being converted to the Kégresse système.

Fig. 51. The Schneider-Citroën armoured car of 1923, which used the Kégresse système.

NATI-3, was of an experimental nature, and was based on a licence-built Ford truck, the GAZ-AA of 1932. This vehicle had a rubber half-track just the same as those applied to the Kégresse series, and during 1933 and 1935 it achieved some success in trials in the Arctic Circle. The impact of the NATI-3 led to a production version, the GAZ-60, which was produced from 1938 to 1942, and finally to the ZIS-42, which was produced for two years, 1942 to 1944 (see Plate 17). Other half-track designs followed based on GAZ-51 chassis and Ural-ZIS/ZIL trucks, but these differed from the original Kégresse ideas.

TRACKED VEHICLES DEVELOPED FOR MILITARY PURPOSES (WORLD WAR I)

I. THE AUSTIN-PUTILOV ARMOURED CAR

As noted on page 85, Adolphe Kégresse successfully applied the half-track principle to a British Austin truck chassis, and from this pilot exercise, the Putilov Zavod conceived a successful cross-country armoured car. This Russian factory had already armoured the Austin 3½-ton vehicle, fitting it with turrets and armament, and by applying the tracked rear axle system a viable war machine was created; altogether 60 such vehicles were produced. Thirty of these Austin-Putilov armoured half-tracks had a single turret with one Maxim 7.62 machine gun fitted, whilst the other thirty units had smaller, twin turrets, each with one 7.62mm machine gun. Details concerning this batch of 60 vehicles have been revealed as conflicting, but the writer has managed to gain some insight as to the probable truth:

Manufacturers:	Chassis – Austin Motor Co., Longbridge Works, Birmingham, England. Armament & Half-Track System – Putilov Zavod, St. Petersburg, Imperial Russia.	
Date of manufacture:	1917.	
	Type 1 (single turret)	**Type 2 (twin turret)**
Length overall:	20ft 7 in (6273mm)	22ft 2 in (6750mm)
Width overall:	6ft 2 in (1879mm)	7ft 10 in (2370mm)
Height overall (measured to top of turret):	7ft 10 in (2370mm)	8ft 10 in (2680mm)
Ground clearance: Ford depth: Tranch crossing: Max. grade:	10in. 2ft 0in. 5ft 9in. 30°.	
Armament:	Twin turret type. Two Vickers-Maxim 7.62 machine guns, one in each turret, mounted either diagonally or side by side with a traverse of 270°. 6000 rounds of ammunition carried.	
Armour Plate:	Up to 7mm max.	
Weight:	5800kg (5 tons 12 cwt).	
Maximum speed:	25kmh (17/18mph), range 80 km (50 miles).	

(See Fig. 52 & Plate 18)

These Austin-Putilov half-tracked armoured cars were very successful, so much so that the Imperial Russian Army issued a directive to the effect that all of the basic types of wheeled cars were to be fitted with half-track assemblies. This occurred in the early part of 1917, but the overthrow of the Czar's government caused the directive never to be implemented.

II. COL GULIKEVICH AND HIS HALF-TRACK ARMOURED CAR

Engineer-Colonel Gulikevich was concerned that existing armoured cars did not possess a sufficient cross-country capability to prosecute their part in the war effort, and in July 1915 he made a report concerning his apprehensions. In this report he stated the following facts: "... The armoured car, which at the moment is the only vehicle used to mount machineguns, is deficient in that it is unable to negotiate every type of

highway – and furthermore, it is easily stopped by barbed wire obstacles; however, we could have a 'tracked-tractor', which is especially designed for moving over all forms of terrain – even ploughed fields. Its special construction ... incorporates one more important feature: that it can break and trample over a barbed wire obstacle." He went on to say that "... if experiments give reasonable results, it would be vital to commence its mass-production immediately. By estimation, I suggest that not less than 40 of these vehicles should be built together, since if we supply the Army in the field with only one or two, the enemy would be able to use and manufacture it in larger sizes and numbers like us."

Obviously, Col Gulikevich had a good grasp of the situation for the British in France did deploy numbers of tanks with some success by surprising the Germans, who could not catch up quickly enough with their own production. Unfortunately, the conditions pertaining to industry in Czarist Russia at that time were such that any form of mass-production would have been impossible, and therefore, Gulikevich named his machine the 'Samodvigately', (meaning 'self-engined' or 'self-propelled') and he originally handed over his report to the Main Artillery Department of the Russian Defence Ministry.

Now, in 1917 Alvin Lombard of Waterville, Kennebec County in Maine, USA had started to fit petrol engines to his patented 'Log-Hauler', and the Russian Government had ordered 104 units of this new type; Gulikevich managed to get hold of one of these to produce his armoured car. He made the vehicle, which is shown in Fig. 52, using the all-metal track-laying system perfected by A. O. Lombard and described in his 1901 US patent; the car as built by Gulikevich also had its front wheels driven to give a maximum traction effect. It was armed with a light gun as well as machine guns. It seems that a number of these armoured vehicles were actually manufactured, and two pictures that are extant show the prototype (Fig. 54) and another, slightly different version in action on a street in St. Petersburg. These vehicles were armoured at the Putilov Zavod.

FULLY TRACKED VEHICLES MADE OR PROJECTED IN CZARIST RUSSIA

One of the first 'tank-like' craft to be promoted in Russia before the Revolution was projected by Vasili Mendeleev between 1908 and 1916, but the design was not put into practice (see Chapter 1). However, another project did come to fruition, mooted by engineer A. A. Porokovskikov who was employed in Riga. His proposition was for a tracked vehicle with a single, wide, track-laying system, and in August 1914 he submitted drawings and details of it to the Military Technical Department of the Russian Government who, subsequently, did not approve it for consideration.

Luckily for Porokovskikov, the Chief Engineer Officer of the North Western Front Army saw some merit in the proposed tank, and he prepared a report on it for the HQ of the Supreme Commander-in-Chief – on 24th December 1914, official despatch

Fig. 52. The Austin-Putilov armoured car (No. 4993 is a military number), fitted with the Kégresse système.

Fig. 53. The armoured car devised by Engineer-Colonel Gulekevich. The tracklaying system was based on the work of Alvin Lombard.

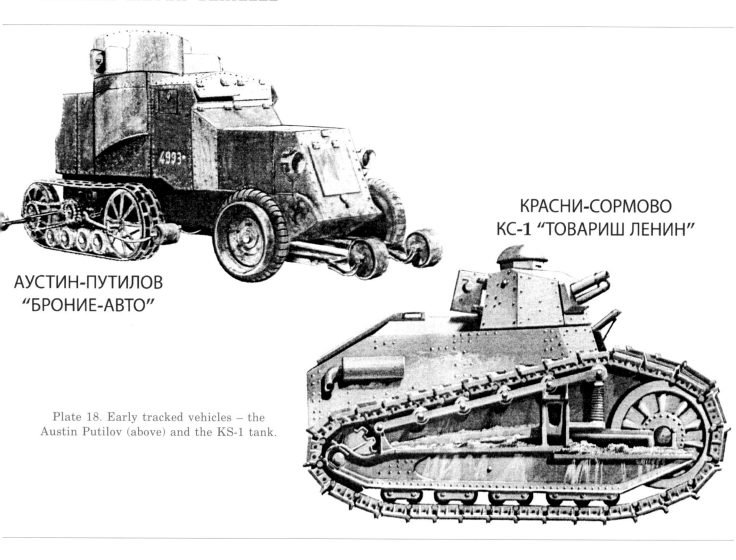

КРАСНИ-СОРМОВО
КС-1 "ТОВАРИШ ЛЕНИН"

АУСТИН-ПУТИЛОВ
"БРОНИЕ-АВТО"

Plate 18. Early tracked vehicles – the
Austin Putilov (above) and the KS-1 tank.

no. 6686 gave permission for the Chief Engineer to construct a prototype. There were two versions given in Porokovskikov's data: one with the single track and another with twin tracks, based on the system patented by the American Benjamin Holt. The single-track version was chosen for manufacture as it was easier to build as a pilot model, and a workshop was erected in Riga in front of the barracks occupied by the Nizhnigorod Regiment.

Work commenced on 1st February 1915, with skilled machinists recruited together with military technicians to ensure that the project was a success. At first a wooden hull was used, without turret or armament, and this was completed by 15th March. Experiments proceeded with a steel hull using a sandwich process, whereby hardened stainless steel was laminated between mild steel to absorb bullet impact. The layout of the chassis with its track system is shown in Fig. 53; a twin steering wheel arrangement allowed the driver to move the frontal part of the single track in the direction he

wanted to go. A 20hp petrol engine mounted at the rear of the chassis drove the rear drive cylinder via a planetary gearing transmission. As the front part of the track could be lifted up to surmount obstacles, the machine was able to travel over any type of ground or remain flat on level surfaces.

A testing area was made at the barracks with the mechanical chassis fitted in the wooden hull; the test took place on 18th March 1915, and certain items were scattered around to provide obstacles for the tank. Unfortunately, these items caused the track to come off. Nevertheless, this problem was soon obviated by the installation of cylinders with sprockets instead of smooth surfaces, and on 20th June 1915 the vehicle was ready for further tests. These were conducted without any untoward event, and the Test Commission published report no. 4563, which concluded that the Vezdekhod was a sound and practical machine. In further tests conducted in Petrograd on 29th December 1915, the 'tank' maintained a speed of 40 versts per hour when ballast simulated the all-up weight of a production version (3½-4 tons). Once again,

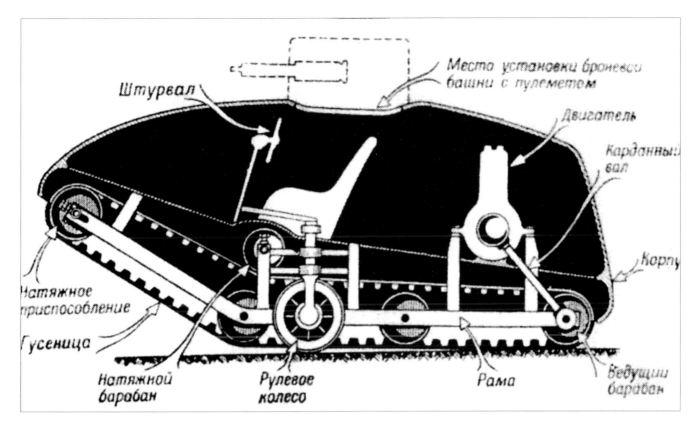

Fig. 54. The fully tracked Vezdekhod designed by A. A. Porokovskikov.

the Czarist mentality caused cessation of the work, as the army expressed little interest in proceeding.

The Russian Government had allocated Ryb.18,000 to subsidise the experiments, but only Ryb.9660 was actually used up, so the inventor kept the surplus. Writing in 1958, Colonel V. D. Mostovenko, a notable Soviet military historian, stated that no drawings of the Vezdekhod appeared to have survived, but some documents revealed sketches and a photograph of the machine. Porokovskikov also promoted a 'Land Cruiser' that consisted of 5 or 6 rollers fitted to separate units, with the machinery housed in the first, and an armoured hull resting on the following units to house the armament, ammunition, and crew. This project was placed before the Technical Committee of the Main Military Technical Department in August 1915, but was not given any authorisation. The official attitude to Porokovskikov's inventions may be summed up in the words of the Chief Engineer of the Main Military Technical Department when he was asked about proceeding with Vezdekhod – "Why should we meddle with this business?"

This official attitude pervaded the Russian establishment, for when other inventors put their proposals before the Main Military Technical Department they received the same treatment. The following schemes were all turned down by the Technical Committee during 1915:

Aleksandr Vasiliev – Proposal for a "large armoured automobile" and introducing tracked and armed vehicles to the army. Refused by the Technical Committee 17th March 1915.

V A Karanski – Proposal for "armoured tractor" with 3 wheels of large diameter. Turned down by the Technical Committee in its report no. 267 of 6th April 1915.

Lieutenant Bikovets – Proposal for "heavy armoured tractor" with eight wheels and a weight of 10 tons, and an engine of 65hp. Refused by the Technical Committee December 1915.

Some of the inventions put before the Technical Committee were of doubtful use, with the latter in the list above being one of them; a large and heavy tractor conceived just for the purpose of crushing barbed wire did seem to be using a sledgehammer to crack a walnut! It would appear that most of the Russian inventors of war machines at that time were obsessed with crushing barbed wire.

III. THE KRASSNII-SORMOVO KS-1 TANK

The first true military tank to be produced in Russia was made just after the Revolution, when the Bolsheviks had gained power. Although this vehicle was produced after the demise of the Czarist regime, the writer considers it pertinent to include, as it was a major step in technical advancement in Russia.

The manufacture of this machine came about after the Soviets were firmly entrenched in the country by January 1918. A newly formed Narodny Kommisariat (Peoples' Commisariat) issued an order that a department be introduced to consolidate all armoured forces into one central command structure. This centre was named Tsentrobron (Central Armoured Bureau), and it became an arm of the Directorate of Military Engineering; from this order the armoured car section was amalgamated with another important group, which was engaged in the construction of armoured trains. By November of 1918 this force had some 150 armoured vehicles to be deployed in 38 platoons, becoming an effective fighting force. Not content with this strategy, V. I. Lenin made a directive that a proper tank be built to enhance the equipment already gathered together. In the autumn of 1919 the President of the National Economic Council of the Soviets, P. A. Bogdanov, following Lenin's instructions, gave the order to commence production.

During the War of Intervention the Red Army captured a number of White Russian tanks that had been supplied by other European nations, and amongst these were a selection of Renault FT infantry support vehicles, taken at Odessa and on the front at Petrograd. One of the tanks that had been snatched near the capital was presented to Lenin himself by the 2nd Ukrainian Soviet Army Group, and this example was later used to provide a basis for the construction of an indigenous machine.

A locomotive building plant at Nizhni Novgorod, the Krasnii-Sormovo Zavod, had been engaged in the repair of captured Renault tanks and had, therefore, some sound knowledge about their constructional details. A design group was formed to undertake the building of replicas. This group consisted of the following engineers: Messrs Khrulev (Director), Krimov, Saltanov, Moskovkin, Chepurhov, Volkov and Yastrbov – all experienced men. The Group realised that complete fabrication of the tank could not be achieved in the one location, for it was necessary

Fig. 55. The Nakashidze/Charron armoured car.

to have specialist factories to provide a contribution. Their plan was to construct a prototype in the army workshops attached to the Krasnii-Sormovo Zavod, and to select other plants to supply specific components. To this end, the Izhorski Zavod at Kolpino supplied the armour and the turret, the AMO Factory in Moscow manufactured the engine and transmission, whilst other, smaller organisations provided sundry parts.

The result of this collaboration was the creation of the 'reverse-engineered' Renault FT M-17 replica fitted with a 37mm light gun and a 7.62mm machine gun. This tank was not, however, a slavish copy of the French machine, for it had the 37mm gun which the original did not possess, and it was not fitted with the stabilizing 'tail'.

The tank was designated the KS-1 (Krasnii-Sormovo 1), and its role was that of infantry support, as was the case with the donor tank. The first unit was completed on 31st August 1920, seven months after the inception of the project, and this first 'native' Russian tank was deployed for acceptance trials at the proving grounds in Kiev. By 1st December 1920, the Soviet Military Industrial Council announced that the trials had been successful and the vehicle was presented to V. I. Lenin. It was also named after the Bolshevik leader, with the appellation 'Freedom Fighter Comrade Lenin'.

At the time of the presentation Lenin declared how the programme for series production was to be implemented, ordering that a further 15 units be made ready for the following spring. However, this was not achieved, but 14 were ready by 1922 and some of these were christened with political slogans, viz. 'Parizhkaya Kommuna' (Paris Commune), 'Ilya Mourometz' (A Russian Hero), 'Krasno Borets' (Red Champion), 'Pobeda' (Victory), 'Burya' (Storm) and 'Proletariat'.

The factory where the KS-1 was assembled, the Krasnii-Sormovo (Red Sormovo) Zavod at Nizhni Novgorod, was founded in 1849, the Sormovo Works being a general engineering plant. Later on, in 1898, these works concentrated on the building of steam locomotives. It completed its 1000th unit in 1905 and continued production of them until 1952. It built 4850 steam engines up to 1941, and thereafter made other types of railway engines.

Another project was also undertaken at the Nizhni Novgorod facility, when a small 'tankette' was developed by an engineer named Maximov. This man proposed a vehicle named 'Zhitonosky' or 'Shield Bearer' in 1919, a 'one-man tank' armed with a single 7.62mm machine gun. It weighed 2¾ tons and was fitted with the AMO-Fiat engine, which gave it a maximum speed of 15mph. The machine gun was mounted at the extreme front of the tank, and its track ran on a series of 10 idler wheels each side, together with a main driver and idler wheel on each side. The Soviet Military Industrial Council rejected the project after a few prototypes had been produced from 1920 to 1922.

The original KS-1-series only appeared to have comprised 30 units, but an improved version, the MS-1 Russky-Renault, was put into production from 1923 onwards. These later machines had greater Russian design input, and formed the basis for the later T-series.

Some specification details of the KS-1 tank have been recorded and these are given hereunder:

The Krasnii-Sormovo KS-1 infantry support tank	
Manufacturer:	The Krasnii-Sormovo Locomotive Works
Date of currency:	1920 to 1922
No. manufactured:	Approximately 30 units (prototype made between 1st February and 31st August 1920).
Engine:	FIAT 4-cylinder, water-cooled, petrol made under licence, AMO works in Moscow
Bhp:	33.5hp at 1500rpm
Hp per ton:	4.88
Length overall:	5 metres (16ft 5in) with tail fitted 4 metres (13ft 1in) without tail
Width overall:	1.75 metres (5ft 9in)
Height to top of turret:	2.25 metres (7ft 5in)
Weight in combat trim:	7 tons (15,432lb)
Armour thickness:	8-16mm
Maximum speed:	8.5kmh (5.3mph)
Range:	60km (37.5 miles)
Trench crossing capability:	1.8 metres (5ft 11in)
Ground pressure:	5.6psi (0.4 kg/cm²)
Max. vertical climb ability:	0.6 metres (1ft 10in)
Max. gradient:	38°

NB These tanks were included on the Russian Army portfolio from 1922 until 1941.

ARMOURED CARS PRODUCED IN CZARIST RUSSIA

Armoured cars appear to have been a speciality of the Russians, for in the early days these vehicles were the most successful military units that they possessed. The story of Russian armoured car design commences with M. A. Nakashidze (see Chapter 2).

I. THE NAKASHIDZE ARMOURED CAR OF 1905

This Georgian invented one of the first armoured cars to be seen anywhere, and he submitted his drawings and designs to the Russian War Department, which after examination did not actually reject it, but stated that it could not be produced in the country. Undaunted, Nakashidze persevered, and his drawings were sent to the French automobile manufacturer Messrs Charron, Giradot and Voight of Puteaux, Seine in order to make a prototype.

An initial order for 36 vehicles was made, but in the event, this was reduced to a single unit. The armoured car, shown in Plate 19, was a particularly effective design, having a good

Plate 19. Early armoured cars – the Nakashidze/Charron
         and the Renault-Mgebrov vehicles.

Fig. 56. The Putilov-Garford armoured car – three-quarter front view and three-quarter rear view.

prove the viability of armoured cars for combat duties. This request did not fall on deaf ears, and resulted in some trials with the Russian Army, held in 1906 in the Oranienbaum area. They commenced with a proving run from St. Petersburg to Oranienbaum, and then on to a small place named Venki; this run took place in close proximity to the capital and, in all probability, started off from the Czar's Palace at Tsarkoe Selo. As there was a Russian Army Military School in Oranienbaum, some machine gun firing tests were included in the trials, and these were organised by the Chief Range Officer of the Imperial Officer Academy at its firing range. Following the success of these initial trials, Nakashidze's armoured car was entered for the army manoeuvres in July of 1906 at Krasnoselo, a location that was also near St. Petersburg.

Reports were also favourable here, for the War Department Commission made the statement: "The armoured car has a wide future as a supporting means of combat." At this point, obviously, Nakashidze must have thought that the future of his proposal was secure, for shortly after the manoeuvres had ended, a plan to upgrade and improve his design at the Izhorski Zavod was suggested; but once again, as had been the fate of other visionaries in Czarist Russia, the War Department eventually rejected the scheme.

Fortunately, records of these trials with armoured cars have survived in the ground clearance, armoured plating 4.5mm in thickness, and a revolving turret housing a machine gun. The basis of the design was derived from experience gained in the fighting in Manchuria, where Nakashidze commanded the Cossack Group. Another two units were added to the order, and when completed the cars were shipped to Russia overland via Germany, where two of the three were 'lost in transit'. Strangely enough, these 'lost' armoured cars later turned up at some army manoeuvres in Germany!

In 1906 Nakashidze submitted a report concerning the deployment of armoured cars to the Russian War Department, in which he requested evaluation tests to be carried out to Central State Military History Archive, and therefore accurate details are preserved. An official photograph of the prototype car fitted with mudguards traversing over the divots at the manoeuvres is reproduced in Fig. 54. The Charron chassis was fitted with a 30hp engine, a specially armoured body carrying a revolving turret with a Hotchkiss machine gun installed, self-sealing tyres, and steel channels on the sides of the vehicle for use in crossing trenches etc. It weighed 3¼ tons, and the mudguards were only present on the prototype. Some authorities seem to intimate that the Russians took delivery of a further nine of these armoured cars prior to the outbreak of World War I.

Fig. 57 (above and opposite). The Austin-Putilov armoured car.

II. THE AUSTIN-PUTILOV ARMOURED CAR OF 1914

Some mention of this armoured military vehicle has been made on page 87 of this narrative, where the half-tracked version was discussed. However, the basic style of the Austin-Putilov car was a wheeled version, manufactured in two distinct types. As previously noted, the vehicle was based upon an English Austin 3½-ton truck, being modified and armoured at the Putilov Zavod. It was the most important armoured car made by the Russians, as most of the rest were but armoured versions of other European and American chassis. The first style of the Austin-based armoured car had four wheels shod with solid rubber tyres, twin turrets fitted with two Vickers-Maxim 7.62mm water-cooled machine guns, and (initially) mudguarding.

These original armoured cars were evaluated at the St. Petersburg Military Automobile School, and one of the experiments carried out was the fitting of special pneumatic tyres, with a mixture of gelatine and glycerine filling the inner tubes. This replacement for air was not a success, and the idea was abandoned.

Details of the two versions of the Austin-Putilov car have survived, and one of the more curious idiosyncrasies of the Russian part of the design was the insistence on two steering positions, the same as was applied to the Russo-Baltic armoured car illustrated in Fig. 21 and discussed on page 30. Originally a wire and bobbin system for the rear steering arrangement was tried, but this was not effective, and two steering wheels directly connected to the front wheels solved the problem.

Specifications of the first and second styles of Austin-Putilov cars		
Manufacturers:	The Austin Motor Co. Longbridge Works, Birmingham, England. The Putilov Zavod, St. Petersburg, Russia.	
Building date:	1914 onwards.	
Basic vehicle:	The 3½-ton Austin petrol-engined truck fitted with twin propellor shafts.	
Engine:	Austin, 50hp, water-cooled petrol engine.	
Armament:	Two Vickers-Maxim 7.62mm machine guns, one in each of two turrets mounted side-by-side. Later versions had the turrets diagonally arranged, but with the same armament. 270° traversing. Approximately 6000 rounds of ammunition were carried.	
Steering:	First model had steering on front axle with forward control only. Second model had a rear steering position as well.	
	First model	**Second model**
Length overall:	15ft 6in	16ft 0in
Width overall:	6ft 5in	6ft 8in
Height:	7ft 10in	7ft 10in
Ground clearance:	15¾in	15¾ in
Armour:	Up to 6mm	6-8mm
Fuel capacity:	15 gallons, 6 pints imperial.	15 gallons, 6 pints imperial.
Maximum speed:	31mph	31mph
Range:	150 miles	150 miles
Crew:	4	5

Initially the Austin Motor Co. did supply completed vehicles but due to wartime commitments the Russians took only chassis and armoured and modified them at the Putilov Zavod. The cars produced in England had mudguards but the Russian examples did not have this luxury. Artillery wheels with pneumatic tyres replaced the earlier solid tyred units.

III. THE RENAULT-MGEBROV ARMOURED CAR

This example of an armoured car was an excellent design, proposed by Cavalry Captain Mgebrov in 1915. It was based on a Renault chassis that was suitably strengthened to take the heavy armour plate, and which had been used previously by the French on their 'Auto-Canon' of 1914, which carried a 37mm gun. This chassis was based on the 18CV passenger car of either type ED of 1913 or type EI of 1914, fitted with a water-cooled, four-cylinder power unit of 4536cc capacity. Steel disk wheels replaced the ordinary artillery type and these were shod with pneumatic tyres, dual at the rear. As the Renault chassis had its radiator situated behind the engine the armoured layout was excellent, with a sloping bonnet able to deflect enemy fire. The vehicle is depicted in Plate 19 (B), where it can be seen to have been a very advanced vehicle for its time; it had twin turrets in a staggered formation, with each one housing a 7.62mm machine gun. Unfortunately, Captain Mgebrov was killed in action later on in 1915 and did not live to see his car completed. However, it was eventually put into production in Soviet days, in 1924. The production versions were made, in all probability, at the Russky-Renault plant in Rybinsk.

IV. THE PUTILOV-GARFORD ARMOURED CAR

This was the largest armoured vehicle devised, manufactured and used in Imperial Russia. The massive, heavily armoured body was constructed at the Putilov Zavod and fitted to an American Garford truck chassis. The main turret faced the rear, and it housed either a 57mm or a 76.2mm assault gun. This latter weapon was of Krupp origin, but was made at the Putilov Zavod. One Vickers-Maxim 7.62mm machine gun was located in the main turret, with two others mounted in sponsons. These vehicles, of which a fair number were built, were also adapted to run on railway tracks. One of these armoured cars found its way as far south as Teheran in Iran in 1915.

Some of the Garford-Putilov type of turrets were also fitted to armoured trains made in the Russian factory. The basis of these armoured cars was probably the Garford model D chassis of 1914, which was a chain-driven, forward-control unit; these were manufactured by the Garford Co. of Elyria, Ohio, prior to its move to Lima, Ohio. An example of this vehicle is illustrated in Fig. 56 and some details of the Garford-Putilov have been recorded as shown opposite.

Fig. 58a. Captain Poplavko's armoured car, and b (overleaf), the second wheeled version of Porokovskikov's Vezdekhod

Manufacturers:	Chassis – The Garford Co., Elyria, Ohio. Armour – Putilov Zavod, St. Petersburg, Imperial Russia.
Chassis type:	Model D 5-Ton Garford of 1914.
Engine:	28/35hp water-cooled, petrol.
Armament:	One 57mm or 76.2mm (Krupp) assault gun Three 7.62mm machine guns (Vickers-Maxim).
Ammunition:	60 rounds main armament. 9000 rounds machine-guns.
Armour thickness:	7 to 9mm.
Length overall:	18ft 9in.
Width overall:	7ft 7in.
Height to top of turret:	8ft 2½in.
Weight:	8.6 to 11 tons (according to arms).
Fuel capacity:	80 imperial gallons.
Max. speed:	11mph on roads. 20mph on rail.
Range:	75 miles.

The Garford-Putilov had chain-drive to the rear wheels only, and was steered from the front only. Wooden artillery wheels shod with solid rubber tyres were fitted.

V. CAPTAIN POPLAVKO'S ARMOURED CAR

This vehicle was a very simple device proposed by Staff-Captain Poplavko of the 7th Armoured Car Brigade of the Russian South-Western Army. In December 1915, this officer proposed that an armoured body be placed on an American four-wheel drive Jeffery chassis with the facility to overcome barbed wire. The shape of the bodywork was such that it could easily crush coiled wire at a speed of about 5mph. A bridge attachment was also employed to cross ditches and trenches. It was tested at the Izhorsky Zavod Proving Grounds in July 1916, where it was quite successful; the trials were carried out over soft and muddy terrain and the car managed to crush barbed wire coils stacked five deep with a coil height of between three and six feet. The Russian War Department subsequently ordered 30 of these cars, and they were supplied, presumably by the Izhorsky Zavod, to form a special armoured car detachment on the south-western front in October of 1916. Poplavko's armoured car weighed 8 tons, had 16mm armour plating, a crew of 5, and the Jeffery chassis was fitted with twin petrol engines. The armament consisted of two 7.62mm machine guns.

An improved version (Fig. 58a) was fitted with box-like armour, and again was based upon the American Jeffery 'Quad' chassis. This car was designated the AB-9, and it had twin engines as before, with two 7.62 machine guns. It weighed 8 tons, had a crew of eight men, and a 5-speed gearbox that could be employed in forward gear or reverse. The length was 19ft 4in, the width 7ft 9in, and the height to the top of the armoured body was about 6ft. Disk wheels with solid rubber tyres were fitted. This was also put into production, as there is photographic evidence of it in service.

The above résumé of armoured cars discusses the more important units that were actually manufactured, either as prototypes or as service vehicles; however, there were several abortive plans that were never put into practice, or proposals that were rejected by the powers that be. One interesting

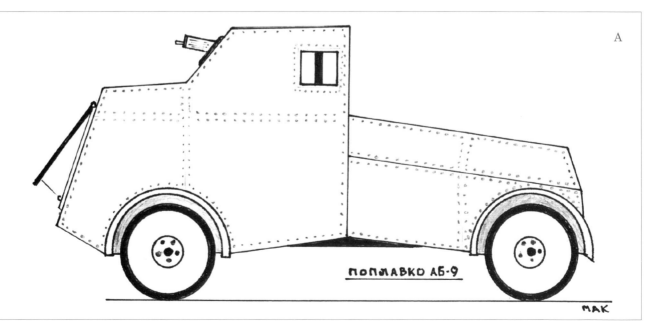

A

ПОПЛАВКО АБ-9

MAK

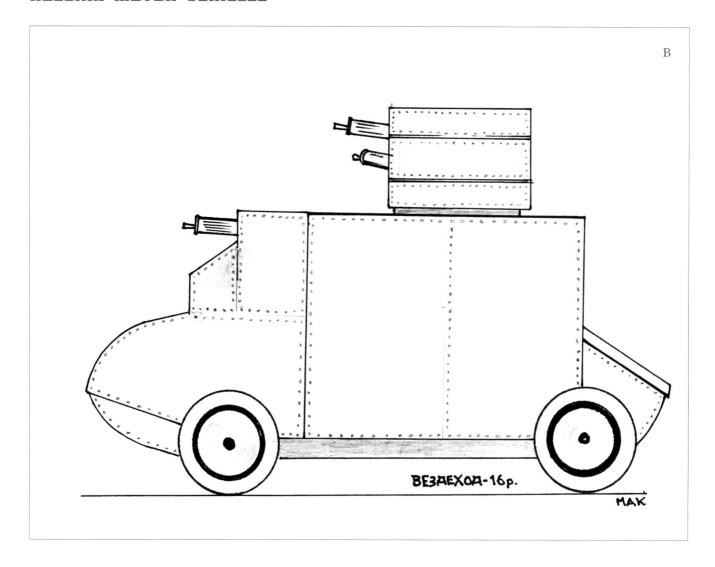

B

ВЕЗДЕХОД-16р.

MAK

proposal was that of the Russky-Renault tank (Fig. 59), mooted in 1915. This project was unveiled in August 1916, and the characteristics were as follows: armoured tracked vehicle, crew of four, 107mm assault gun (probably of Krupp design), 20 tons all-up weight, a 200hp power unit, and 10/12mm armour plate. The project was initiated by the Russky-Renault Zavod in Rybinsk, and presented to the Technical Department on 10th August 1916 only to be rejected in the normal way!

VI. POROKOVSKIKOV AND HIS 2ND VEZDEKHOD
Engineer A. A. Porokovskikov had already produced his original Vezdekhod design by 20th June 1915, only to have it rejected at the eleventh hour (see page 90). Nevertheless, some more thought was given to it by the Chief Engineer of the Main Technical Department of the Russian War Ministry, because there was a distinct lack of any progress towards making a Russian tank by the winter of 1916. The Chief Engineer ordered

Porokovskikov to develop his original 1914 project further, if only to allay adverse public opinion at the time. A new Vezdekhod was constructed, and it was ready for tests by 19th January 1917.

The new design was given the designation "Vezdekhod 16r" to distinguish it from the first effort, and it was a combined track and wheel machine. Like the first it had the track concealed within the hull, and this mechanism consisted of a rubber track system that revolved on four spring-loaded 'drums'; the rear drum actually operated the track by means of a transmission arrangement driven by a petrol engine. One drum was the front idler, whilst the other two carried road wheels at their extremities, mounted outside the hull. These wheels were ordinary automotive disks, and the front two steered the machine when on paved roads. Sprung suspension at the front enabled good obstacle climbing ability, and all four wheels had pneumatic tyres.

The way the second Vezdekhod worked was simple; when

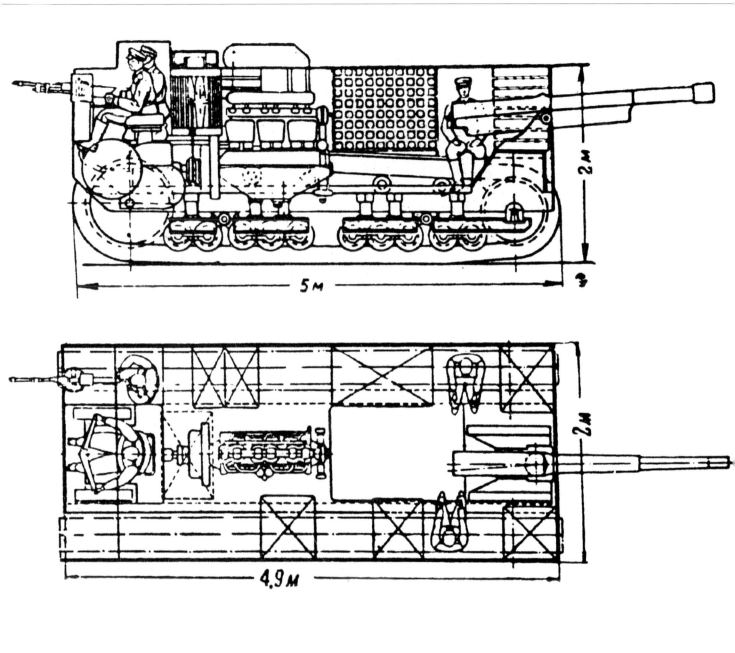

Fig. 59. Line drawing in sectional plan and elevation of the proposed Russky-Renault armoured vehicle.

running on paved roads or other smooth surfaces it was driven like an ordinary car, but if the wheels sank into soft ground, the track took over and the vehicle continued on the track alone. If the track only was needed to be used then the road wheels could be lifted clear to enable this form of traction to be used. Three or four machine guns made up the armament and two of these could be mounted in the turret; the others were placed at the front of the vehicle. The car was divided into two parts with a metal bulkhead in between. The fore part contained the drive, the controls and the forward machine guns, whilst the after compartment housed the mechanical elements of the vehicle. The Vezdekhod 16r is illustrated in Fig. 58b.

Fig. 60. The Czar Tank. This is believed to be the only surviving picture of the vehicle.

THE FINALE, THE LARGEST MILITARY VEHICLE IN THE WORLD

The final vehicle to be investigated is the pièce de resistance of all Czarist efforts in the scope of military transport engineering – the Czar Tank.

This fantastic machine (Fig. 60) was the largest military vehicle in overall size ever produced (the Maus, the German World War II tank, was the heaviest). It was a miracle that it was ever produced at all, or that it was ever accepted for construction, even as a prototype.

The story goes that the Russian Minister of War, Lebedenko, approached Czar Nicholas II with a proposition for a military machine that would easily break through the German lines in World War I, and that would allow Imperial Russia to be victorious. He demonstrated a model of this 'engine of war' to the Czar, who became enthusiastic about the project and authorised him to supervise it in order to produce a full-sized prototype.

Lebedenko gathered together a group of famous scientific and mechanical personalities to commence building his brain-child, including Professor Nikolai Ye. Zhukovsky, 'The Father of Russian Aviation', Professor Steckin, later to become a member of the USSR Academy of Science, and Alexei Mikulin, the well known aero-engine designer; he also procured a grant in the sum of Ryb.210,000 from the Imperial Russian State Treasury in order to finance the work.

The specification drawn up by Lebedenko described a vehicle in the form of a tricycle fitted with two very large, 10 metre diameter road wheels at the front end, and a 2000mm diameter roller at the rear; he estimated that with wheels that large, the machine would be able to travel over trenches, ford streams, climb over buildings and other obstacles with ease, and weigh something in the region of 60 tons.

The construction of the Czar Tank was overseen by the Main Military Technical Department, and work on components for the machine began in great secrecy at a workshop on Khamovnik Ploshad in Moscow. These parts were removed for assembly to a forest clearing by the Orudiev Marshalling Yard, near the town of Dmitrov, north of Moscow. The build was finished by the August of 1915, and the resultant 'tank' resembled a large gun-carriage, with spoked wheels 9 metres in diameter, together with a rear roller for steerage. A lattice steel girder framework supported the front end, and also the turret which contained the armament. Power was supplied by two Sunbeam 'Maori II' 240hp aero-engines, one to drive each road wheel independently, and to assist in steering the vehicle. Unfortunately, under test it appeared that the Czar Tank was an unwieldy affair that was very difficult to control; it was moved to the railway yard where it moved forwards very slowly and ended up demolishing a stand which was in front of a large tree, where it came to a halt, embedding its

roller in mud. A suggestion at the time was made to employ a larger diameter roller to enhance the accuracy of the steering, but this idea was dismissed by the Technical Department, which was becoming tired of the contraption and forbade any more time and effort to be expended upon it. The machine was abandoned forthwith, and it languished in the railway yard until well after the war, eventually being cut up for scrap in 1923.

Notwithstanding the problems encountered with the operation of the Czar Tank, its construction does say a lot concerning the ability of Russian engineering at the time, for the building of wheels nearly 30ft in diameter, with approximately 120 tension spokes, was no mean feat. Alexei Mikulin was disappointed with the outcome of the trials of this strange machine, for he considered that the large diameter road wheels made the invention superior to any tracked vehicle, even though the Czar Tank weighed 40 tons and it had a high ground pressure on its three points of contact.

CONCLUSION

The writer has endeavoured to utilise his research into the Russian motor industry as a whole to portray the efforts of the pioneers in the years before the 1917 Revolution. From the foregoing narrative it may be seen that there was no lack of talent or ingenuity on the part of Russian engineers, craftsmen or scientists. Men such as Professor N. Ye Zhukovsky, K. E. Tsiolkovsky, who set out the parameters for space exploration, and Professor Yuri Lomonsov, the famed railway engineer, all contributed hugely to the scientific knowledge of the day, whilst craftsmen such as Pyotr Ilyin and Pyotr Freze, both excellent designers and engineers, manufactured superb carriage-work, with the latter personality co-operating in the building of the first all-Russian motorcar in 1896. Most of the information contained in this work has never been put together before to provide an overall picture of the Czarist motor industry, and the writer has spent 30 years garnering details concerning it. A prolonged visit to the Soviet Union during the 1970s revealed a considerable amount of data that had never reached these shores, and visits to other European countries has consolidated this data over the years.

The AMO F-15 passenger car – the first such vehicle to be designed and built in Russia after the demise of the Czarist and Provisional Governments.

APPENDIX

LIST OF THE MAIN ENGINEERING WORKS CONCERNED WITH VEHICLE PRODUCTION

THE IZHORSKY ZAVOD at Kolpino, near St. Petersburg – A large general engineering facility established in the 19th century. Situated just south of the capital.

THE PUTILOV ZAVOD, St. Petersburg – The premier engineering works in Czarist Russia. Established in 1805, it manufactured all manner of products including steam locomotives. 2577 units were made between 1894 and 1930. In 1918 the factory was renamed the Krasnii-Putilov Zavod (Red Putilov Works), which changed in the 1930s to the Kirov Zavod, after Sergei Kirov, a Politburo member who was assassinated in 1934.

LIST OF TYRE MANUFACTURERS FROM 1900 TO 1917

TVO PROVODNIK, Riga, Latvia – One of the best tyre manufacturers in the world at that time. The quality of their tyres was extolled all over Europe and even in the USA.

SHIN TREUGOLNIK (Triangle), St. Petersburg – The other Russian tyre maker; this firm made solid rubber tyres, rubber tracks for the Kégresse système, as well as pneumatic tyres.

LIST OF AERO–ENGINE MANUFACTURERS IN CZARIST RUSSIA

THE AKSAI AGRICULTURAL IMPLEMENT FACTORY Rostov-on-Don (Gnome).

THE ELEKTRO-MECHANICAL WORKS LTD., Deka brand.

GNOME-RHONE AIRCRAFT ENGINE WORKS, Moscow (Fili).

PYOTR ILYIN LTD., Moscow. Sunbeam engines under licence.

T KALEP – THE MOTOR CO. AVIATION DEPT, Riga (later to Moscow).

NATIONAL AIRCRAFT ENGINE WORKS, Kherson.

RUSSO-BALTIC WAGON WORKS (RBVZ), Riga.

RUSSKY-RENAULT FACTORY, Rybinsk.

SOCIÉTE DES MOTEURS SALMSON, Moscow (Fili).

COMPONENT PLANTS

SINGER SEWING MACHINE CO., Podolsk (Magnetos).

It is also believed that a subsidiary of the ZENITH CARBURETTOR CO. operated in St. Petersburg.

BIBLIOGRAPHY

BOOKS WITH RUSSIAN TEXT

Aviatsiya b Rossii (Aviation in Russia), M. V. Kellaysh, G. P. Svishchev & S. A. Kristianovich, Izdatelstvo* Mashinostroenie, Moscow – 1988.

Avtomobile Strana Sovetov (Soviet Automobiles), L. M. Shgurov & V. P. Shirsov, *Izdatelstvo* Dosaaf, Moscow – 1958.

Automobilia Vestures Lappuses (History of the Automobile), E. Leipins, Zinatne, Riga – 1983 (Latvian text).

Istoriar Kirovsko Zavoda (History of the Kirov Factory), S. Kostuchenko, I. Khrenov & U. Fedorov, Izdatelstvo Mayal, Moscow – 1966.

Ot Samobegloii Kolyaski do ZIL-111 (Early Days to ZIL-111), A. S. Isaev, Izdatelstvo Moskobskii Rabochii, Moscow – 1961.

Istoria Putilovsk Zavod (History of the Putilov Works), M. Mitelman, B. Glebov & A. Ylarnsky, Moscow – 1961.

Kratkii Avtomobili Spravochnik (Automobile Data Book), Izdatelstvo Avtotranizdat, Moscow – 1963.

Tank (Tank), A. S. Antonov, Izdatelstvo Voenizdat, Moscow – 1947.

Tanki (Tanks), Col. V. D. Mostovenko, Izdatelstvo Voenizdat, Moscow – 1958.

MAGAZINES WITH RUSSIAN TEXT

Tekniki Molodezhni – Soviet popular science journal.

Za Rulyem (The Driver) – Soviet motoring magazine. Various issues.

Avtomobil – Soviet technical automotive journal.

MAGAZINES WITH CZECH TEXT

Auto & Moto Veteran, no. 7, 1987 – Organ of the Bratislava Veteran Car Club.

Automobil – Czech motoring journal (various issues).

NEWSPAPERS WITH GERMAN TEXT

Dresdener Anzeiger – 7th December 1910.

Automobil Revue (Swiss) – December 1974.

BOOKS WITH ENGLISH TEXT

Russian Civil & Military Aircraft 1884-1969, Heinz Nowarra & G. R. Duval, Harleyford Publications / Argus Books Ltd., Watford – 1970.

Russian Tanks 1900-1970, John Milson, Arms & Armour Press, London – 1970.

Armoured Trains of the Soviet Union 1917-1945 Wilfried Kopenhagen, Schiffer Publishing, Atglen, Pennsylvania, USA.

MAGAZINES WITH ENGLISH TEXT

Autoexport Round-up, no. 68 to 87 – English language house journal of V/O Avtoexport, Vokhonka 14, Moscow.

NB: Other bibliographical notes may be found in the text of this work.

* 'Izdatelstvo' indicates publisher.

BIOGRAPHICAL NOTE

Alexandr Nikolaivich Zakarov (left) produced most of the colour drawings that appear in this book. A talented technical artist, he was in great demand during the days of the former Soviet Union.

Zakarov worked for the leading Russian scientific and technical journals, and teamed up with motoring historian and engineer Lev Shugurov to produce a series of illustrated articles that appeared in the house magazine of the Russian trade organisation V/O Avtoexport. Other pictures were drawn for the motoring journal *Za Ruylem* (The Driver), and for the popular science magazine *Teknika Molodezhni* (Young Technician), which was similar in format to the American publication Mechanix Illustrated. Having a keen interest in motorsport, Zakarov was involved with the racing team known as the Moscow Auto-Road Institute (MADI), as well as the All-Union Scientific Institute.

INDEX

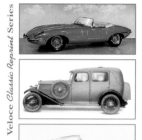

Veloce Classic Reprint Series

THE COMPLETE
CATALOGUE
OF BRITISH
CARS
1895-1975

DAVID CULSHAW & PETER HORROBIN

The Rise of Jaguar

A detailed study of the 'Standard era' 1928 to 1950

Barrie Price

A study of how SS metamorphosed into Jaguar, how the company prospered and grew (even during the world's worst economic depression), and the importance of the Standard Motor Company. Many hitherto unknown facts disclosed. Copiously illustrated with superb and evocative contemporary photographs.

Hardback • 25x25cm • £37.50 • 176 pages • 265 pictures • ISBN: 978-1-904788-27-0 • UPC: 6-36847-00327-2

Tel: +44 (0) 1305 260068 • Email info@veloce.co.uk • Prices subject to change • P+P extra

BATTLE CRY!
Original Military Uniforms of the World

Soviet General & field rank officer uniforms: 1955 to 1991
(land, air, border & intelligence services)

VELOCE

Adrian Streather

...parade, dress, service and field uniforms worn by Soviet Generals and field rank officer... ...es, MVD (internal army), KGB intelligence and Border Guards from 1955 to 1991, when... ...ed. Also acts as a collector's/buyer's guide as well as providing ancillary information on... medals, awards and graduation badges.

...k • 24x20cm • £14.99 • 128 pages • 150 pictures • ISBN: 978-1-84584-267-3 • UPC: 6-3684...

www.veloce.co.uk/www.velocebooks.com